Eldership Oversight in the 21st Century:

Factors contributing to decline

Eldership — Oversight in the 21st Century

Factors contributing to decline

Mike R. Roberts
Doctor of Ministry

This study is dedicated to my best friend and the love of my life –
my wife, Terri Sue Roberts. She encouraged me to stay the course,
when many times I wanted to quit. And to my daughter who proofed
many papers when needed and stayed out of the way when I was
having my fits. Both have helped me to stand firm
on the Word of God and to remain steadfast in the faith.

Contents

Chapter One: Research Focus

Chapter Two: Review of Relevant Literature

Bibliography

Appendices

Foreword

Michael Roberts addresses some very significant questions and needs for the 21st century elders or shepherds of the Lord's church in *Eldership Oversight in the Twenty-First Century: Factors contributing to decline*. He deals with a very critical issue in the body of Christ: a lack of young men who aspire to be shepherds of the flock of God. In fact, it is so critical that the church is in spiritual ICU. He has done a tremendous job in the research needed to draw proper conclusions and make vital recommendations for the future of the church. He truly presents shepherds who are God's servants in feeding, protecting, loving, knowing personally, and laying down their lives for the flock (Acts 20:28-32). Mike truly supports the biblical model of the shepherds in the church.

The problem addressed in this book is the patterns and factors contributing to the decline in eldership oversight in the twenty-first century. He identifies these patterns and factors that contribute to the decline of church leadership. This study will also make recommendations on how to change these patterns and return to a biblical form of leadership within the body of Christ. He argues for a major change in how shepherds are identified, qualified, and perform their responsibilities in a return to the New Testament pattern as given in 1 Timothy chapter 3 and Titus chapter 1. He believes the inspired word in teaching that shepherds are a must for the growing congregation in the twenty-first century.

The theoretical thread of this book is "What is the current state of the eldership oversight in the twenty-first century? Many congregations today lack qualified elders, and many do not desire elders. Many congregations do not have men in training to be elders. Many of those who are elders (shepherds) are installed, not because they are scripturally qualified, but because they are good CEOs and successful in the secular realm. Today, many Christians do not give elders the respect and honor that the Bible gives them. Many men today are scripturally qualified to be shepherds but do not desire the job. The lack of qualified elders in the twenty-first century has had a weakening effect upon the body of Christ and needs to be studied so that a solution may be found." He answers the why from his many years of experience in local church ministry and qualitative research among churches in Oklahoma and Texas with and without elders.

Mike, with respect for adequate research, is positive about presenting the facts of the present day leadership in the church and the bright future ahead. Shepherds and prospective leaders who will read this book according to Mike's definitions, goals, concepts, and recommendations will grow and glorify in God in all things pertaining to the spiritual life of the body of Christ. He well deserves the recognition of authoring this much needed book!

Roger E. Shepherd, Dr. of Missiology
Associate Professor of Turner School of Theology
Amridge University, Montgomery, Alabama

Acknowledgments

This book was made possible by the gentle and caring guidance of my Amridge University Dissertation Committee; the loving and ever-encouraging presence of the Porter church of Christ members; and my elders who continually encouraged me to push forward as they patiently listened to lesson after lesson based on the thing I was studying in class.

Therefore, I want to express my deepest appreciation to Dr. Roger Shepherd, my mentor and my dear friend who has taken me under wing and helped me walk through this process for the last 2+ years, always the encourager. I also acknowledge Dr. Cynthia Guy and Dr. Eric Dishongh for reading, guiding, encouraging me, and for being patient with me during the research and writing process. I also want to acknowledge Terry Brackett, Pat Boyd, Roy Cole, and Roy Essary–the Porter church of Christ elders–for giving me the necessary time and backing to not only work on this book, but also preach the undiluted Gospel of Jesus Christ. I also want to thank the nine congregations represented in this study and the thirty individual Christians who offered their valuable insights and knowledge of elderships in the churches of Christ. Without their honest response and insights this book would not have been possible.

I also humbly thank my God for blessing me with the support system of family and friends needed to complete this research, and more so for the opportunities He has given me to serve in His Kingdom, allowing me the privilege and honor to be a minister of the Gospel. If nothing else is known of me, *"Remember me, O my God, for good."* (Neh 13:31)

Abstract

Roberts, Mike R. 2017. "The Current State of the Eldership Oversight in the Twenty-First Century: Some Factors Contributing to Decline" Amridge University, Turner School of Theology. Doctor of Ministry.

The problem addressed in this book is the patterns and factors contributing to the decline in eldership oversight in the twenty-first century. The churches used in this study are in the states of Oklahoma and Texas. Data collected consists of two parts. In the first, members of the church participated in both surveys and interviews to provide insight into their perception of the current and past leadership status. Then, two case studies were done, one in a congregation with a current eldership and one without. The second part of the study was to determine what patterns contributed to the decline of the numbers of congregations with elderships. In the last two chapters of this book I will present the patterns found in the study and make recommendations.

The methodology used is the grounded theory study within the qualitative method, using surveys and interviews to identify and analyze the data showing the patterns contributing to the changes in leadership. Two case studies were used to confirm these patterns and changes. This included surveys and interviews of thirty participants from nine congregations of the churches of Christ. The case studies consisted of one congregation which had an eldership and one which did not. These case studies were conducted to establish how elderships are maintained or lost within the current state of the congregation.

The goal of this study is not only to identify patterns and factors which contributed to the decline of church leadership, but also to make recommendations on how to change these patterns and return to a biblical form of leadership within the body of Christ. With the proper leadership structure in the church, the spiritual health and growth of the church will follow.

It is my conclusion that the factors which contributed to the decline in eldership oversight must be changed if the church is to grow in spirit or in number. I also believe that the proper eldership oversight with its biblical origin is an important means by which the church of Christ can maintain a healthy future of existence in an ever-changing world.

Mentor: Dr. Roger E. Shepherd

Chapter 1:

Research Focus

The focus of this research is to identify problems contributing to the decline in church leadership and give recommendations to restore its biblical form. Chapter one will present the introduction with the statement of the problem, the purpose of the study, delimitations, and assumptions. Chapter two will include previous research and literature review on the topic of leadership in the church. In chapter three I will discuss the procedures and research methodology to be used in this research, the research subjects, the questions asked, how the data will be collected, and the procedures for analyzing that data. Chapter four will give the analyzed findings from that data. Chapter five will offer conclusions drawn from the findings of that data, as well as the implications established from those findings.

Personal Background Story

Having been born in 1962, I have a unique perspective. I have seen a time of great growth within the churches of Christ, as well as times of apostasy. I was born into a family of which there are thirteen gospel preachers. My grandfather was an elder (shepherd) for my entire life, a true man of God who constantly studied and taught the Scriptures to all who would listen. He was both mentor and friend to many a young preacher and called many of the great warriors of God his friend. It is within this context that I have seen a change in church leadership. I have watched as the shepherds of old were true leaders, leading by a life of servitude, then witnessed the new breed come to power as the CEO of the congregation. I have seen the leadership change from one who was loved and respected, to given no authority whatsoever. Now the time has come when finding scriptural leaders in a congregation is very rare, if the congregation has elders at all. In fact, many congregations would rather have business meetings to decide the issues.

In 1987, I was sitting in a small church listening to a young preacher preach on the "Grace of God." He began telling how God's grace was bestowed upon us regardless of our desire to be recipients of it. I remember thinking that he could not prove, by the Bible, what he was teaching. Then I watched as one of the elders, a man who was seventy-nine years old with little education but a lot of Bible knowledge, went down and asked this young preacher to please have a seat. This aged elder began at the same passage that the young man had started with and preached correctly the "Grace of God." After he was through, I watched as this old elder and this young preacher embraced and cried together at the power of the Gospel. Later, the elder explained that he had to fix that problem then and there, lest someone leave thinking what was being taught was true and miss heaven. Since that day, I have heard a lot of error taught from pulpits, yet have not seen an elder stand up and stop the teaching.

Statement of the problem

In the last few years, there has been a change in the oversight of the body of Christ. I plan to research the question, "What is the current state of the eldership oversight in the twenty-first century?" Many congregations today lack qualified elders, and many do not desire elders. Many congregations do not have men in training to be elders. Many of those who are elders (shepherds) are installed, not because they are scripturally qualified, but because they are good CEOs and successful in the secular realm. Today, many Christians do not give elders the respect and honor that the Bible gives them. Many men today are scripturally qualified to be shepherds but do not desire the job. The lack of qualified elderships in the twenty-first century has had a weakening effect upon the body of Christ and needs to be studied so that a solution may be found.

Purpose of the study

The purpose of this study is to identify factors that have contributed to the decline in eldership in the body of Christ found in the Southern states of Texas and Oklahoma. Specifically, the strengths and weaknesses will be examined in an effort to ascertain the spiritual maturity of the shepherds currently in leadership. This study will help the current elderships to grow in their spiritual formation and learn what needs to be overcome to strengthen that leadership which, in turn, will strengthen the church. Has the body of Christ become weak in the areas of both numerical and spiritual growth, as well as spiritual knowledge, due to the lack of elders to mature them?[1]

Research questions

The steady decline of spiritually mature shepherds in the Lord's church has become problematic. While the number of congregations without shepherds has grown, the question of why this has occurred needs to be studied. Within the leadership, the mentoring process that we see in the Bible is not being experienced in many of the congregations in the body of Christ. These shepherds have lost some of their ability to lead in the spiritual formation of the congregation. The leadership ability of the shepherds who lead the church today is going to be examined. There are some questions which lend themselves to be asked and answered, such as:

1. *Why has the number of congregations without elderships multiplied?*

2. *What have the elderships today lost in the ability to mentor the next generation of elders? And what are the implications for the church today?*

---

1   Aubrey Malphurs and Will Mancini, *Building Leaders: Blueprints for Developing Leaders at every Level of Your Church*, (Grand Rapids: Baker Books, 2004), 10. Malphurs not only contends that there is a leadership problem, but that the problem is one of developing leaders.

3.   *Why have the elderships today lost the desire to mentor the next generation of elders? And what are those ramifications?*

4.   *Why has the eldership today lost the ability to lead congregations in their spiritual formation? What affects has it had on the local congregation?*

Delimitations

In this proposed study, elders will only be looked at in the boundaries of leadership in the Lord's church as it already exists. I will not be discussing the context of the qualification of elders, although some of the qualifications may be mentioned as they apply to the various questions being asked.[2] This will not be a study based upon the leadership as designed by man or various denominational hierarchies, but rather, leadership as it was designed by God. This will not be a study of evangelistic or pastoral leadership as the world has devised, but, again, it will be focused upon the biblical examples of leadership as taught by the writers of the New Testament.

The scope of this study will be limited to selected churches of Christ and selected leaderships within the churches of Christ to establish if there is a discernible difference between the leadership in the church today as compared to the church of yesterday. There are enough congregations and elders who have seen both this century and the last to allow the picture of leadership from both time frames to be compared. This study will not be looking back into the centuries prior to the 20th century, or the history of what that leadership was like. Only that which is observable through interviews will be included in this study. That will limit the time frame from the 1970's to the present, because there are still members from that time period and former elders who possess knowledge of past leaderships.

---

2   A comprehensive list of biblical elder qualifications may be found in Appendix B.

Definitions of key terms

Within this study, there will be some general terminology which the reader must understand in order to have a complete comprehension of the research. These terms are defined below:

> *Pastors, elders, shepherds, overseers, and leaders*: These will be used as synonymous terms, all describing the individual or group of individuals (when used in the plural sense) whom the Lord has made overseers of His church (Acts 20:28). Sometimes these men, as a group over a congregation, will be referred to as an eldership.

> *Office of Bishop*: This is used in the King James Version as an interpretation of the Greek word " επισκοπον." According to A. T. Robertson, though the use of the word "office" is not used in the original text, the term επισκοπον means "over-seership."[3] Marvin R. Vincent states that "while it did not come through Jewish tradition, it seems to have come to use in a quite natural way."[4] He states that "just as 'πρεσβυτερος' passed into official designation through the natural association of authority with age, so to the word 'επίσκοπος' would also be, almost inevitably the designation of a superintendent."[5] It was used in conjunction with officers of the army and those who were the overseers of workmen. So, in the context of 1 Timothy 3:1, the overseers of the body of Christ also have the authority to oversee and to have the rule over those within the body.

> *Church of Christ*: This term will be used to describe the organization which Christ established at Pentecost and

---

3   Archibald Thomas Robertson, *Word Pictures in the New Testament, vol. IV The Epistles of Paul* (Nashville: Broadman Press, 1931), 572.

4   Marvin R. Vincent, *Word Studies in the New Testament* (Mclean: MacDonald Publishing Company, 1888), 227.

5   Ibid.

purchased with his blood, not a denominational organization which was built and established by man. It will also be used interchangeably with the term "body of Christ."

Spiritual Formation: This term will be defined as the transformation of the spirit in light of the spirit which is found in Christ. It is the maturing of the Christian because of the Word of God taking an active part in the life of the believer. This "spiritual formation" can take place on an individual basis, as well as in a congregation as it matures by strong spiritual teaching.[6]

Mentoring: This term is to be used for the process of teaching and instructing an individual by one who is more mature and spiritually formed in the ways of God. It is the biblical method of helping young men to become qualified to one day take on the leadership role of overseeing the church. It is done by both instruction and observation of one who is already mature in Christ (1 Cor 4:16-18).[7]

Biblical: This term is defined as those things relating to the Bible teaching on any subject.

Culture: This term is used to define a way of thinking, behaving, or working that exists in a group, place, or organization.

Ethics: This refers to a standard of right and wrong, good and evil, which is believed in as God has given in the Bible.

---

6   Aubrey Malphurs, *Advanced Strategic Planning* (Grand Rapids: Baker Books, 2005), 80-92.

7   Paul D. Stanley and J. Robert Clinton, *Connecting: The Mentoring Relationships You Need to Succeed in Life* (Colorado Springs: Navpress, 1992), 133.

Morals: Morals are the standards one lives by, whether right or wrong, good or evil, what one actually does, regardless of their belief.

Assumptions

In this study, it is assumed that members of the body of Christ know, understand, and agree with the qualities of the men that the Bible views as shepherds as they are listed in 1 Timothy chapter 3 and Titus chapter 1. It is assumed that the church wishes to have the leadership of the local congregation as prescribed in the Bible and not under a pastoral system as established by men in the denominational religions. However, it will be shown in the study that many congregations are ruled by a pastoral system. The pastoral system is a form of leadership in which the minister (preacher) is in charge of the congregation.[8] However, in the Bible, the term pastor is used in defining the shepherd.

Review of literature

The material I looked at from Kenneth Boa has the premise of using God as the ultimate example of the perfect leader and then applies that to the leadership of the local church. I agree with Boa when he shows that our values are based on God. In the research, these are the values to which every leader will be compared. If there is any loss in the ethics and morals of the leadership in the twenty-first century, there would have to be a departing from the values God has shown. As we try to determine what has been lost in eldership oversight in the twenty-first century, it must be known what was obtained in the past. Boa gives a good look at what the perfect leaders should be. He shows the integrity which elders should possess in order to be the proper leaders. He discusses the character of the leader and that character is something which comes from the inside out. He states that "character is not a matter of

---

8   Catherine Soanes and Angus Stevenson, *Concise Oxford English Dictionary* (New York: Oxford University Press, 2008), 1047.

outward technique but of inner reality."[9] Boa shows a biblical picture of "Two-Way Communication," how that Solomon, in the book of Proverbs, warns of the problems of "one-sided communications" and how to avoid them. Boa also discusses the "Barnabas factor" and how that hope may be sustained when leaders effectively offer words of support and comfort.[10]

Lynn Anderson, in his book, has a lot of valuable information on the qualities of the leadership in the body of Christ. One of the main points is that an elder is to be a "mature spiritual guide."[11] This is an excellent book on mentoring, what it is, and how to perform the task in such a way as to help the leaders of tomorrow become spiritually minded. It uses Jesus as the example for equipping the saints and helps one to understand that even Jesus was not able to make disciples of all men, and not even He was able to have an "unlimited number of intimate relationships."[12] The author does a nice job of showing an overall look at what shepherds should be when they possess a strong spiritual foundation. Anderson also states that "healthy churches have enough shepherds to maintain authentic, intimate shepherd/flock relationships."[13] This is a relationship which the Bible stresses over and over, yet many churches today do not have elderships. How to multiply the leadership is one of the key principles of maintaining this balance of leaders and followers.

Brian Croft wrote a book which deals with the leadership's effect on the church. He states in his introduction that "we suffer from an identity crisis."[14] Unfortunately, he misses his definition of the term "pastor." While his book discusses qualities, which are appropriate for the shepherd, he often uses the term "pastor" to describe the evangelist

---

9   Kenneth Boa, *The Perfect Leader: Practicing the Leadership Traits of God* (Eugene, WIPF & Stock Publishing, 2006), 30.

10   Ibid., 190.

11   Lynn Anderson, *They Smell Like Sheep, vol. 1, Spiritual Leadership for the 21st Century* (New York, Howard Books, 1997), 125.

12   Ibid., 93.

13   Ibid., 175.

14   Brian Croft, *The Pastor's Ministry: Biblical Priorities of Faithful Shepherds* (Grand Rapids, Zondervan, 2015) 11.

(preacher).[15] Many of these qualities do apply to the evangelist, yet Croft is placing the evangelist in the place of the shepherd (elder). He discusses the fact that many have forgotten the job which they are called to do. He also explains that the shepherds, as well as the evangelist, must guard and protect truth. In a day when subjectivism and relativity are common cries, the lack of standing for truth is seen. Shepherds must guard the flock which they lead. Croft shows how this is done not only by example but also by teaching.[16] He also shows that by their knowledge of truth and speaking that truth, they will have to confront sin. He reminds the reader that, while at times speaking the truth may hurt the individual, "the truth has the power to set us free, then the best thing you can say to someone is a word that will bring conviction to their heart."[17] Croft addresses one of the same responsibilities as Anderson, the training of future leaders. He states that, concerning the call of a leader, after months of discussion, praying, and member meetings, we vote to affirm the call.[18] In this context, I don't believe it is biblical for men to decide if God actually "called" someone to the leadership or not. However, Jesus tells us in Matthew 7:16-20 that "by their fruits ye shall know them," so we recognize eldership qualities of a man by his actions.[19] Croft also states that "it takes a pastor to recognize a pastor."[20] In the first chapter of *Ministry is...*, David Early tells us that we can know those with the qualities of the servant by the "cloud of dust" they leave.[21] Comparing men's lives to the Bible will always show who possesses the qualities to be shepherds. Croft also explains that "God appoints leaders to be inter-

---

15   Ibid., 37.

16   Ibid., 164.

17   Ibid., 131.

18   Ibid., 172.

19   It should be understood that many of Croft's ideas are based on his denominational understandings and not Bible principles. If one applies the pastor principles to the elders (pastors) instead of the preacher, they would be biblical in nature. In Ephesians 4:11, Paul uses the term pastor (*poimen*) which is also translated shepherd in Hebrews 13:20 and 1 Peter 2:25.

20   Croft, *The Pastor's Ministry*, 176.

21   David Earley and Ben Gutierrez, *Ministry is ...: How to Serve Jesus with Passion and Confidence* (Nashville, B&H Publishing Group, 2010), 7-9.

cessors, those who represent the needs of the people to God."[22] I agree that we can give supplications and petitions to God on behalf of our brethren. Overall, this book has a lot of information on the leadership of the church when it is all put back in the proper context.

When looking at these books together, I can get an idea of how the eldership oversight, shepherding the flock, and the steps that were used to replicate themselves in the next generation were being implemented. Seeing how many of these authors lived and studied during the twentieth-century also give me a great comparison for the eldership oversight seen today. If I analyze the literature at hand and compare it to the way eldership oversight is conducted and replicated today, I should be able to come to an understanding of at least some of what has been lost.

Research methodology

The leadership in the body of Christ is the context of this study. God has given biblical examples and commands of how the leaders of His church should conduct themselves in all situations of life. By the leader's conduct, he serves and oversees the church. This study will be conducted by working with nine selected churches of Christ (five in Texas and four in Oklahoma) to assess the spiritual health of their individual leaderships and memberships. The study will consist of interviews with thirty people, ranging in age from thirty-two to eighty-four, both men and women. The only qualification is that they must be members of the church of Christ in either Texas or Oklahoma. Most of the participants were members in the twentieth-century and would have a knowledge of local church leadership in both centuries. Those in the study will be selected out of congregations with and without elderships. As a result of this study, it is hoped that the current situations may be changed, and there can be a revival of the spiritual formation of the leadership within the body of Christ.

The research for the problem under discussion will be qualitative in nature. Qualitative research looks at characteristics and qualities of

---

22   Croft, *The Pastor's Ministry*, 61.

various patterns with all nuances and complexities.[23] I will be looking at the qualities of the eldership oversight within these selected churches of Christ, how those leadership qualities compare to times past, and what has changed if there is found to be a change. I will be looking at the shepherds, as well as the job being done by the shepherds. The research will be conducted in the real-world setting, to ascertain what conditions exist in the eldership oversight of the church today, and to compare that data to what is known about the church of the past. Paul D. Leedy and Jeanne Ellis Ormrod state that "all qualitative approaches have two things in common. First, they typically focus on phenomena that are occurring or have previously occurred in natural settings, that is, in the 'real world.' And second, they involve capturing and studying the complexity of those phenomena."[24]

The eldership oversight of the twenty-first century contains both of these aspects. The collection of data is for the purpose of trying to find factors and patterns that contributed to the decline in leadership found in the church today. The data collected will show me what this present-day setting is and why. The method being used within the margins of qualitative research will be a *grounded theory study*. Grounded theory study "is to begin with the data and use them to develop a theory. The term *grounded* refers to the idea that the theory that emerges from the study is derived from and rooted in data that has been collected in the field rather than taken from the research literature."[25] During the interviews and surveys, we will try to ascertain how the congregations perceive the work of the leadership and the shepherds themselves. These interviews should allow the subjects to express themselves in such a way that the data may show their perceptions of the leadership oversight. In this part of the research, I will be trying to ascertain what the congregation has experienced in the various forms of leadership oversight. With this method, it should be possible to begin understanding any change which might have taken place in both attitude and spiritual

---

23 Paul D. Leedy and Jeanne Ellis Ormrod, *Practial Research, Planning and Design, 11th ed.* (Old Tappan, NJ, Pearson, 2014), 251.

24 Ibid.

25 Ibid., 256.

formation within the leadership of the twenty-first century. This method was chosen because of its ability to show how any change of eldership oversight has affected them as individuals and how it has affected the congregation.

During this study, there will be the need to establish many new contacts. These new contacts will open the door for the interviews and surveys needed to collect the data for this study. I will conduct interviews with elders and congregation with whom I am familiar, and also with elders and congregations whom I have yet to meet. This will produce a well-rounded base in which to gather the data. There will also need to be a rapport established with these subjects in order to gain a sense of trust, so that the lines of communications may be open.

Case studies are used to validate my findings. A case study is when an in-depth look is given to any individual, program, or event for a set period of time. The case study method is going to be used to examine what the eldership of the twenty-first century does within the study groups in the selected congregations. Once this is determined, the data will be compared to what is known about the eldership in the twentieth-century, as found in the interviews with those who lived through those years and reviewed what is found in literary resources. I will be looking for patterns of the leadership oversight with whom the research is being conducted and comparing this to what was in the past. I will also be looking for what the spiritual formation of these elders is today compared to what has gone before. It is with this method that much of what was written in the past will play a part in showing the historical aspect of how the church was overseen. The outcome of that type of leadership, compared to what is being done today, or the lack of leadership all together for those congregations which have no shepherds, will be a priority. This will be done by questionnaire and interviews of the participants in this study.

Implemented jointly into the study, there will be a combination of interviews, surveys, and a study of historical writings of the past to find the necessary data about what is different in eldership oversight. The subjects will be mixed between laymen and shepherds, both men and women from congregations of Texas and Oklahoma. I will use these methods to study thirty people of various ages and the congregations (of various sizes) which they lead. The age differences of the elders should give us a reading of the difference in priorities and spiritual formation of the elders themselves in the twenty-first century. It has been reported that the younger leaders today have not only lost some of their leadership skills, but also the ability to replicate themselves, resulting in a depletion of leaders in many congregations.[26]

Summary

In summary, due to my present knowledge about elders, it is easy to see that there has been a change in church leadership. This change is also pointed to by Wilson, Ferguson, and others as the patterns have moved away from the biblical examples. Many local congregations do not have elders. Others may not want elders to guide them. I will be using qualitative research in the form of a grounded theory study. This type of study will be used because it uses existing data to form a theory of what created the problems. Then case studies of selected congregations will be used to either confirm or reject those findings.

The review of literature, found in chapter two, shows many aspects of leadership which has been researched. In the literature review I will summarize and synthesize the information as needed for a better understanding of the existing knowledge of the leadership, as well as the shortcomings already recorded. Comparing the problems of today with that of the past should give us information needed to help reestablish biblical leadership within the body of Christ.

---

26 Malphurs and Mancini, *Building Leaders*, 10. Malphurs' teaching experiences over the last twenty years prove that while there are many potential leaders available, the church is not training them to become elders. As a result, we now have a leadership crisis in which current leaders do not know how to train future leaders. In addition to Malphurs, several other authors call attention to the current eldership decline. In 1997, John Wilson - in a speech at Pepperdine University - addressed the leadership crisis and the fact that today's elderships show little resemblance to the biblical model of leadership.

Review of Relevant Literature

Chapter two is a review of literature and research data which has already been studied on the leadership role. It will take into account mainly religious leaders, but at times, will compare secular leaders as it applies to the development of the overall understanding.

With the growing number of congregations without shepherds as well as the number of congregations with weak elderships, it is essential to understand why this situation has occurred. Many of the scholars on the subject of leadership have shown the need for the mentoring process. However, some of the modern shepherds have lost their ability to lead in the spiritual formation of the congregation which makes it difficult to develop the next generation of shepherds. With the shepherds losing their ability to lead in the spiritual formation of the congregation, more and more congregations have gone to a men's business meeting structure instead of the biblical type of church leadership.

Leadership decline

There are many reasons for leadership decline found in the religious world. One in particular is the loss of legitimacy. The loss of legitimacy has been reported to bring about a mass defection of members. The legitimacy of any leadership should always remain at the forefront of the leadership's goals. It must be remembered that legitimate authority or power is not the same as leadership. Legitimate power exists because of the role or office leaders occupy, while leadership is a trait which can come without the office. Many shepherds today are set in an office by which the scriptures give them legitimate authority, but they do not have the leadership skills needed to shepherd the flock. It was this same lack of leadership from the deterioration of the congregation which John Maple wrote about in his article, "Discord in the Mother Church."[1] Gilbert W. Fairholm attributed the leadership decline to the focus on small special group tactics, rather than on the big picture of the communal needs.[2] According to Anderson, it is also thought that these same leaders work more as a CEO and refuse to allow the members to take an active role in the work of the organization.[3] Part of the problem in the loss of legitimacy can be found in the loss of the spiritual maturity of the leadership. It must be remembered that leadership of any organization, especially the church, is based upon the soul of the man. How sensitive the shepherd is to the congregation's need to grow, change and mature will determine how well he is able to lead that congregation. The Bible example of leadership always comes back to the shepherding analogy, because a flock is not in need of managers, but rather someone out front leading. With the new style of leadership being of a managerial mindset, the decline seems inevitable.

Another symptom of the leadership decline is the fact that few shepherds are trying to replicate themselves. There have been many volumes written on the mentoring processes and the need for leaders to take a proactive role in seeking the men who will replace them when their tenure is over. Even in the business world this seems to be the norm. Many leaders are afraid to train or make room for new blood, out of fear of the competition. Paul D. Stanley and J. Robert Clinton pointed out that one of the reasons that mentoring has been declining, and thus creating the decline in qualified shepherds, is that many fear the transparency that comes with mentoring.[4] There is a sense of account-

---

1   John T. Maple, "Discord in the Mother Church: The Failure of Leadership in the Later Years of the Church of Christ in Baker Gate, Nottingham," *Restoration Quarterly* 55, no. 4 (2013): 215.

2   Gilbert W. Fairholm, *Capturing the Heart of Leadership: Spirituality and Community in the New American Workplace* (Westport: Praeger Publishers, 1997), 95.

3   Anderson, *They Smell Like Sheep*, 34-35.

4   Stanley and Clinton, *Connection*, 20.

ability that many do not like and feel that it leaves one vulnerable as the mentored learns the inner man with all of his frailties and insecurities. It is through the mentoring process that the ebb and flow of spiritual maturity is nurtured. If done correctly, this process will last the individual a lifetime. Stanley showed how this is especially important for the thirty-five to forty-five-year-old men who would be shepherds. This is an age which is confusing both spiritually and secularly, and has a need for guidance and stability to be mentored. Stanley continued, saying that "a key to good coaching is observation (when possible), feedback, and evaluation. An experienced coach does not try to control the player (or mentored), but rather he seeks to inspire and equip him with the necessary motivation, perspective, and skills to enable him to excellent performance and effectiveness."[5] Aubrey Malphurs lists mentoring as one of four types of leadership training and explains that prospective leaders should be pro-active in seeking out a mentor in which to form a personal relationship.[6] Malphurs lists the four training methods as: 1) Leader-driven training, where believers take responsibility for their own growth; 2) Content-driven training, which focuses on the transfer of knowledge; 3) Mentor-driven training, where the member works closely with a mentor or coach; and 4) Experience-driven training, based on hands-on and expertise. It was also advised that many leaders, when asked to be a mentor, will initially refuse; however, the mentee should not take "no" for an answer and continue to pursue the needed help.

Transformational Leadership

Because of the movement away from the biblical example of church leaders, there is a need for transformational leaders. Transformational leadership is defined as leadership which "seeks to change the status quo by articulating to followers the problems in the current system

---

5   Ibid., 76.

6   Aubrey Malphurs, *Maximizing Your Effectiveness: How to Discover and Develop Your Divine Design* (Grand Rapids: Baker Books, 2006), 145.

and a compelling vision of what a new organization could be."[7] Transformational leadership is based upon six validated factors. Bernard M. Bass identifies these factors as: (1) articulating a vision, (2) providing an appropriate model, (3) fostering the acceptance of a group goal, (4) high performance expectations, (5) providing individualized support, and (6) individualized consideration, as validated by Podsakoff, MacKenzie, and Moorman.[8] While it is unscriptural to try to change the organization of the body of Christ from the biblical example, it is only right to change poor structure back to the first century example. It is within this context that the transformational leaders are needed. They need to establish the ability to communicate with the congregation and show them the vision of God and how He views the church. The transformational leader will influence change back to the biblical style of organizational influence on the individual, the organization, and the community round about him. In this style of leadership, the relationship between the leaders and the congregation is a long-term concern as are the goals which are set.

While transformational leaders are interested in change, it is not change for the sake of change which the shepherds of the Lord's church look for. Instead, it is a change from the world's view of morals and ethics to the spiritual view which is found in Christ. Paul said it best when he wrote, "Let this mind be in you, which was also in Christ Jesus." (Phil 2:5) Flavil Yeakley also agrees that one of the most important failures in the leadership today in the body of Christ is that of a failure of communication.[9] Transformational leaders are great communicators and able to envision the congregation with the goals that have been planned by that leadership. Yeakley states that "telling is not the same thing as communicating."[10] He also says that most elders desire

---

7   Robert N. Lussier and Christopher F. Achua, *Leadership: Theory, Application, & Skill Development* (Mason: South-Western, 2013), 331.

8   Bernard M. Bass and Ruth Bass, *The Bass Handbook of Leadership Theory, Research, and Managerial Applications Fourth Edition* (New York: Free Press, 2008), 625.

9   Flavil R. Yeakley Jr., *Church Leadership & Organization* (Nashville: Christian Communications, 1986), 27.

10   Ibid., 28.

to know that they have the congregational consent on any given topic, but most go into the eldership without the communications skills which would let them know that they have that consent. It is unfortunate, but the possibility of a reduction in numbers of members due to the transition back to the biblical model is likely. However, research suggests that this would only be a temporary reduction in numbers until the spiritual maturity of the congregation could be elevated as a part of the change. In fact, Erica Dollhopf records research that shows the negative impact from leadership transitions weakens over time: "Therefore, a short-term time frame may show more discernible effects of leadership change than a longer time frame would be able to demonstrate."[11] In her chapter on moderating factors of leadership transitions, Dollhopf shows that an overlap in leadership also can have a negative impact upon how well that transformation takes place.

Dealing with the culture

Another aspect of transformational leadership is how to operate at an effective level amidst the culture of the day. It is often reported that in order for a congregation to grow, it must conform to the culture. Bryan D. Sims and J. Paulo Lopes claim that in order for this change to occur, leadership must change its focus from transforming the individual to concern over the congregation. They state, "In this respect leadership catalyzes adaptive work, not by making changes happen, but by evoking change dynamics among people who work and learn together. The focus on leadership, then, shifts from the individual as a leader to the action of leadership that fosters creative and productive learning within organizations. Thus, leadership is fundamentally a system phenomenon."[12]

---

11   Erica J. Dollhopf and Christopher Schetile, "Decline and Conflict: Causes and Consequences of Leadership Transitions in Religious Congregations," *Journal for the Scientific Study of Religion* 52, no. 4 (December 2013): 679.

12   Bryan D. Sims and J. Paulo Lopes, "Spiritual Leadership and Transformational Change Across Cultures: The SLI Leadership Incubator," *Journal of Religious Leadership*, vol. 10, no.2 (Fall 2011): 63. The thought here is based on the findings from R. Marion and M. Uhl-Bien, "Leadership in Complex Organizations," Leadership Quarterly 12(4) (2001): 389-418 and expressed by Sims and Lopes.

While studying several Jesus movements, including the first century church, Alan Hirsch established what he calls the Missional DNA. It consists of six basic elements which he claims is present in every stage of the disciple's life. These elements are: 1) Jesus is Lord; 2) disciple making; 3) missional-incarnational impulse; 4) apostolic environment; 5) organic systems; and 6) communitas, not community.[13] Missional DNA, according to Hirsch, changes the culture, which is the biblical concept, instead of changing the leadership to meet the needs of the culture. For instance, in the DNA the first element is Jesus is Lord. This is a simple confession which every believer must make in order to be obedient to the Scriptures. The second element is that of disciple making. According to Hirsch, it is a core principle of the church. It is here that Jesus made His focus and where all missional movement must begin. However, in Matthew 28:19 Jesus gives this as an individual responsibility to all who would follow Him. The third element (missional-incarnational impulse) as described by Hirsch is the outward thrust of Christians to leave the building of worship and go into the community to make disciples of all. This again, is an individual responsibility in which the culture of the community is changed to conform to the Gospel. The fourth element, the apostolic environment, shows that each individual needs to dwell within Christ in order to be a part of Christ. Sims and his colleague indicate Hirsch believes that the true apostolic influence is characterized by a more bottom-up, highly relational quality of leadership rather than the typical CEO-type leadership, that tends to disempower others.[14] With this being the case, Hirsch's opinion would definitely show a more biblical type of leadership style of servant leadership, as Jesus demonstrated in Matthew 20:20-28. In the fifth element (organic system), Hirsch tries to characterize a living system in which the Body of Christ attempts to mirror life itself. The final element (*Communitas*) is found to be more than the "community" with which the culture today

---

13   Alan Hirsch, *The Forgotten Ways: Reactivating the Missional Church* (Grand Rapids: Brazos Press, 2006), 24-25.

14   Sims and Lopes, 72. Sims and Lopes are using the findings of Hirsch as found in his book, *The Forgotten Ways: Reactivating the Missional Church* (Grand Rapids: Brazos Press, 2006), 163.

is accustomed. Hirsch said that "the persecuted church in both the early Christian movement and in China experienced each other in the context of shared ordeal that binds them together in a much deeper form of community than the one we have generally become accustomed to."[15]

While there are some significant differences in this form of leadership, the research still lays some credence to the transformational leadership in which the congregation works as a whole once members have been transformed into the likeness of Christ. Transformational leadership transforms both leadership and follower alike, one person at a time until the body becomes united in Christ. This brings about a change in the community as well, by allowing the light of the Gospel to show through the members of the congregation.

Authentic spiritual leadership

While looking at the research on "Leadership," it is extremely important to notice the difference that is found between secular and spiritual leadership. Spiritual leaders were defined in one article as "knowing God's will, walking in it, and effectively soliciting others to follow" (2 Tm 2:2). Many books and studies have been conducted with this definition in mind. Most of these will not be a part of the research for this book as the delimitation will exclude the basic attributes listed for spiritual leadership found within the Bible. But here it is useful to see what the research has to say about the authentic spiritual leaders and in understanding why many have left this form of leadership style.

In Richard L. Mayhue's article, he notices that when a group of "pastors" were asked to define spiritual leadership, their answers focused upon the leader. They have a tendency to ignore the spiritual aspect of leadership. This would seem to reinforce the idea of why many congregations today focus upon the CEO type of leaders, instead of the servant type of leaders. Many of today's shepherds have business degrees with hours of training in the secular realm on how to manage a corporation. These men are seen as being successful in handling money and in their worldly business practices. Few, however, are taught how

____
15   Hirsch, *The Forgotten Ways*, 218.

to be the servant and how to lead the flock by being out front leading the way, as they teach and train those who would follow. Mayhue shows that God has a far superior plan in leadership. He notes that God gave a blueprint which includes: 1) an inward set of qualities, 2) a pattern of life by which one must live, 3) righteous motives and inappropriate actions, and 4) fruitful outcomes.[16] These are the same attributes which are found in both 1 Timothy 3:1-7 and Titus 1:6-9, and from which many books have been authored. It is also interesting to know that when spiritual leaders voluntarily accept their role within the church, it not only helps them to become spiritually more mature, but also helps them to maintain their ability to mentally function better. R. David Hayward and Neal Krause suggest that those who were involved in higher levels of religious activities showed a reduced presence of functional impairment.[17] The attributes shown in the spiritual leader can also be recognized in the servant leader, as well as the transformational leader as they are closely aligned, both of which focus on the leader-follower relationships. Robert K. Greenleaf explains that the servant leader is a servant first and then a leader. He says that "it begins with the natural feeling that one wants to serve, to serve first. Then conscious choice brings one to aspire to lead."[18] Michael Burch and his colleagues conclude that "the strong areas of agreement between leaders and followers involved administrators' personal attributes-beliefs rather than practices. Those qualities perceived to be less practiced, the mentoring and developing faculty and staff along with the encouraging, motivating and empowering of faculty and staff, were of an interpersonal nature and would be dependent upon the leadership support to be successfully implement-

---

16   Richard L. Mayhue, "Authentic Spiritual Leadership," *The Master's Seminary Journal* 22/2 (Fall 2011): 217.

17   R. David Hayward and Neal Krause, "Voluntary Leadership Roles in Religious Groups and Rates of Change in Functional Status During Older Adulthood," *Journal of Behavioral Medicine* 37, no. 3 (June 2014): 543-552.

18   Robert K. Greenleaf, *Servant Leadership: A Journey into the Nature of Legitimate Power & Greatness* (New Jersey: Paulist Press, 1977), 27.

ed."[19] It is from this vantage point that the need for qualified (spiritual) leaders is seen. Alexander Strauch states, "The most common mistake made by churches that are eager to implement elderships is to appoint biblically unqualified men."[20] This mistake has compounded the problem of church leadership to the point that many congregations are now opting for no eldership and for men's business meetings in lieu of biblical leadership. This is one of the many reasons that the church is in need of spiritual leaders. J. J. Turner states that "if the church is ever going to accomplish the mission given to her by God, it must have spiritual leadership."[21] It is because the church in its very nature as well as its purpose is spiritual, that its leadership attributes must also be spiritual. Turner goes on to say, "The challenge is to control them (his natural qualities) by the inward, spiritual man. Through dedication to God, the leader seeks to handle properly his natural leadership qualities. In the hands of a spiritual man, they take on a new meaning and application."[22] When an eldership is spiritual by nature, then a congregation has men worth following as they lead down the paths of righteousness.

Bob R. Agee's article discusses the use of servant leadership as an effective type of leadership within the church. He uses a biblical definition of the servant leader and discusses how this type of leader both knows and understands not only the congregation but the mission and purpose of the group of people they are to lead. Agee breaks down the ways of effective servant leadership into eight different areas of work. The conclusion found was that leaders would be leading their flock regardless of the circumstances which they face. This thesis includes a great variety of relevant resources for suggested reading.[23]

---

19 Michael J. Burch, Patricia Swails, and Randy Mills, "Perceptions of Administrators' Servant Leadership Qualities At A Christian University: A Descriptive Study," *Education* 135, no. 4 (2015): 403.

20 Alexander Strauch, Biblical Eldership, *An Urgent Call to Restore Biblical Church Leadership* (Littleton, Lewis and Roth Publishers, 1995), 68.

21 J. J. Turner, *Christian Leadership Handbook* (West Monroe: Howard Publishing Co., 1982), 145.

22 Ibid., 145.

23 Bob R. Agee, "Servant Leadership as an Effective Approach to Leadership in the Church," *Southwestern Journal of Theology* 43, no. 3 (2001): 7-19.

Globalization and leadership

The data collected by Jack Barentsen was used to examine the new forms of leadership found today. This data shows how these new forms of leadership have been produced by phenomena such as globalization, technology, and the development of a knowledgeable and network society, just to list a few. This data was collected by the study of ancient historical contexts as well as by qualitative interviews with various pastoral leaders of three different countries. Barentsen concluded that the broad societal changes are bringing about a new type of identity model of leadership being influenced by the social, religious identity and that these leaders connect this to the church's role within the society. This article is based upon a world view of church leadership and prescribes to change the leadership to fit the culture instead of changing the culture to fit the church.[24] In a biblical study of leadership, cultural influence is not the key ingredient to leadership, rather the biblical leader changes the culture.

Organizational influence

The data found in the article *Shifting Images of Church Invite New Leadership Frames,* by Sharon Henderson Callahan, is based upon the work of several men (James Kouzes and Barry Posner at the forefront), as well as the work of seminaries in Washington state. This data showed that how the church is viewed influences how the leader will lead. This research was conducted in two ways. First, a random survey was taken in Western Washington, and second, data was collected by students in the author's classes in pastoral leadership at Seattle University's School of Theology and Ministry. The data suggests that curriculum needs to be developed that will help current leaders develop the next generation of leaders. This research supports the idea that leaders are viewing the church as communal, striving to serve the community and struggling to

---

24 Jack Barentsen, "Church Leadership as Adaptive Identity Construction in a Changing Social Context," *Journal of Religious Leadership* 14, no. 2 (September 2015): 49-79.

transform itself into a discipling body. It also invites others to explore and develop a more effective means to train these new leaders.[25]

The data used by Mark E. Dever, is from lectures of the Dallas Theological Seminary, and is designed to determine what impact ecclesiology has in the church today, as teachings of the church are examined in leadership, membership, structure, culture and character. Using various surveys and polls through selected Baptist congregations, as well as looking back at historical records, data was collected for a comparison to find how much influence the local ecclesiology taught dictates the belief of the local congregation. The findings in this study will show that the doctrine of the church is very important because the church is to be the "appearance" of the Gospel. While the findings of this study are sound and are confirmed by others, it is a shame that the doctrine Dever teaches is faulty, for the only Gospel found is that of the Bible.[26]

The data of Erica J. Dollhopf and Christopher P. Scheitle used for this study was taken from the 2006-2007 National Congregations Study, first administered in 1998. It was used to determine the cause and consequence of leadership change upon the size and health of the local congregation. This qualitative study was given as two cross-sectional surveys or as a panel survey of various congregations. It was given to a small sample of the original 1998 samples as well as a full new sampling of congregations. The findings of this study give evidence that many different complexities of leadership transition differ between the secular realm and the religious realm. There are many common denominators. The understanding of these denominators can help to better plan for the process of leadership change and keep damage to a minimum during these transition periods. This study helps define the need for leadership development to be conducted within the local congregation, as well as the need for better understanding and controlling the membership decline in the aftermath of congregational transition. While looking at the

---

25   Sharon Henderson Callahan, "Shifting Images of Church Invite New Leadership Frames," Journal of Religious Leadership I, no. 1 (2002): 78-79.

26   Mark E. Dever, "Ecclesiological Issues for the Local Church Today," *Bibliotheca Sacra* 172, (October-December 2015):387-397. Dever looks at pastors as being ordained preachers who lead the congregation. The Bible uses the term pastor for the elder and not the preacher.

declining leadership in the Lord's church, these findings may help identify some of the initial causes of the decline.[27]

Everett Ferguson used the data of his research to examine both the authority and tenure of elders as found within the New Testament survey of both scripture and history. Ferguson believes that by examining the interrelationship of abilities, service, and leadership, it is possible to establish the authority and tenure of elders. Case studies show four organizational structures known to be used in New Testament times. These include the monarch (Roman), democratic (Greek city-states), oligarchic rules (rule by a few) and finally the Jewish elder-system, in which the body is made up of unequal members but with each given a place in a functioning body. This last governing body was shown by the data to be the type of leadership seen in the first-century church. Ferguson's article agrees with many others in the field that church leadership prescribed in the biblical text is for the congregation to follow the leaders who are to lead and not lord over the body. This data also helps to show that elders are to be servants in this form of leadership.[28]

Church in transition

Deloris E. Harris-Harrison used research data to examine the challenges of churches in transition in their cultural context and diversity of their multicultural needs. This study was conducted by using three churches of various denominational backgrounds and cultures to ascertain what type of leadership strategies would be required in order to function properly with the multicultural backgrounds of each. This information was gathered by conducting interviews with members of each congregation. The conclusion of this study was that while each congregation was different in nature, the problem remained the same. This problem relates to how the pastors of each congregation as the transformational leaders influence the lives of those whom they serve.

---

27 Dollhopf and Scheitle, *Decline and Conflict*, 675-697.
28 Everett Ferguson, "Authority and Tenure of Elders," *Restoration Quarterly* 18, no. 3 (1975):142-150.

This article supports the need for the congregation to understand the leaders and the diversity in which they serve.[29]

Leadership and the aged

Data from the study by Hayward and Krause was used to examine how the leadership position of laypersons affected both the functioning and severity of physical limitations in older adults. It used three waves of data collected from surveys conducted by face-to-face interviews with peer groups of 1) older adults who regularly attend religious services, 2) older adults who do not regularly attend a religious service, and 3) those who regularly attend, and hold lay leadership positions. The findings pointed out that those older adults who held lay leadership positions in their congregation had a slower decline in their functions of physical limitations. It underscores the fact that those who are stronger in their leadership duties tend to have a longer active service for God. While this study hinted that the self-awareness of one's leadership role has an impact on the outcome, it does not look at the spiritual maturity of the individual as to whether that has any bearing on the outcome.[30]

Kenneth Holderread used data produced from the Pacific Region of the Association of Clinical Pastoral Education meeting to explore the influence of spiritually mature elders on the community in which they worked. The case study involved three individuals who, while engaging in leadership roles, were not officers or officially designated as elders. They were chosen because of their spiritual maturity in handling themselves as they did indeed have a productive influence over the meeting by helping it to move forward. The finding of this study showed that one of the most important roles of the "pastor" (elder) is that of facilitating the lay person to grow spiritually and developing them into elders themselves. This article gives validity to the mentoring process and the

---

29   Delores E. Harris-Harrison, "Leadership Challenges of Churches in Transition: A Study of Three Churches," *Journal of Unification Studies* 13, (2012):175-190.
30   Hayward and Krause, *Voluntary Leadership Roles*, 543-552.

influence that is given by those who are spiritually mature to those who are striving to follow in their path.[31]

Leadership and church growth

Data from the study of John Maple explored the effects that the leadership of various congregations of churches of Christ has upon the growth of the church to discover whether congregations can overcome an intransigent leadership.[32] This study used the record books from the local congregations in the area of Nottingham (Baker Gate and Sherwood Street primarily) showing how the leadership handled the splintering effects of personal disagreements within these congregations. However, many congregations today have split over this very problem. While the "presidents" (elders) are the primary subjects seen in these minutes, congregational members are also seen in the disagreements and chaos which is often recorded. The findings pointed to the fact that as long as the leadership was steadfast in their opinions, the schisms remained. However, when each member of the leadership was willing to be flexible in the areas of opinion, then reconciliation was found. These findings agree with other sources (including the Bible) that even in the eldership of the body of Christ, leaders must not place their own needs above the needs of others. To be a good leader, one must first be the servant. One of the shortfalls of this article is the failure to point out that in matters of doctrine; one must remain steadfast at all cost.

The study by Mayhue, discussed earlier, is based upon the need for "Authentic Spiritual Leadership." The author prepared this article to bring to light the attributes needed to recognize true spiritual leaders.

---

31   Kenneth O. Holderread, "The Role of Eldering and The Christian Community," *Brethren Life and Thought* 24, no. 4 (1979): 205-209.

32   Maples stated that "unfortunately, due largely to new leaders' lack of 'the spirit of grace,' discord and conflict-even to the point that three splinter groups broke off from Baker Gate between 1866-1872-rendered the congregation incapable of functioning as a mother church." When a leader is intransigent then he is unwilling to change his views or to agree with those who oppose him. This is a sinful attitude to have unless one is dealing with doctoral aspects of the church. In matters of opinion one needs to be willing to give and take.

These attributes were based on data collected from outside sources, as well as his own qualitative studies and scriptures. The author concluded that the strong natural leadership (SNL) is one who was sufficient, submitted, spiritual, and steadfast. The article supports the finding of others that in order to be biblical shepherds, they must have the attributes that are found in the Scriptures and that must be taught to the next generation of leaders. In doing so, it is not only possible to identify the SNL, but they can be trained up and created.[33]

Derek Penwell produced the data found within his survey of the leadership in the Christian Church as it relates to ministers and elders vying for the power of leadership. Using a survey of the history of the Stone-Campbell movement and the development of the lay leadership found within that time frame, the author compared that data to what is now taking place at the First Christian Church in Middlesboro, Kentucky. The three views of ministry found in this study were then compared to find out how the changing role of the elders in the Disciples of Christ has come about in the last century. It was found that there is a standing rift between what existed in the Stone/Campbell movement and what the Christian Church practices today. This study found that there should be a movement within that denomination to relocate the ministry back into the hands of laity instead of a leadership of ordination. Comparing this to other works, the findings of the historical survey of the Stone /Campbell movement shows how they tried to restore the New Testament principles of an elder, deacon, and ministry form of self-government, while the Christian Church departed for a denominational type of ordination, in lieu of a local self-government.[34]

The data in Burke Rochford's and Kendra Bailey's article was collected over an eleven-year period for the purpose of understanding the factors which influence the success, decline, and/or failure of new religions.[35] They quoted Rodney Stark's thought that new religious groups

---

33 Mayhue, *Authentic Spiritual Leadership*, 223.

34 Derek Penwell, "The Changing Role of Elders in the Disciples of Christ," *Lexington Theological Quarterly* 35, no. 2 (2000): 62-82.

35 E. Burk Rochford Jr. and Kendra Bailey, "Almost Heaven: Leadership, Decline and the Transformation of New Vrindaban," *Nova Religio* 9, no. 3 (February 2006): 6.

succeeded only as far as the legitimate leaders' authority allowed them to effectively advance the spiritual growth and purposes of the New Vrindaban movement (a renegade Hare Krishna community).[36] In this qualitative study of eleven years, the senior author visited the West Virginia community in which fieldwork was conducted on a yearly basis for days at a time. This was to interview key leaders as well as a dozen residents, and others who at one time were devotees, but had since left the community. This study concluded that because of the loss of legitimate leadership power of the founder (Kirtanananda Swami), as well as the loss of funding and the transformational goals, the community faced decline and failure. This article underscores the need for any organizational leadership to maintain a sense of legitimate leadership power and authority recognized by the whole of the organization.[37]

Data from the state of West Virginia and from the country of Brazil have been used to examine the three organizational principles of the Spiritual Leadership, Inc. and whether they are able to be transferable in the world context of the various congregations. The author used several case studies to examine whether these principles could derail the declining memberships of aging congregations, while establishing newly resurrected leaderships and congregations. These case studies were conducted using three declining Methodist churches from Huntington, West Virginia. The data from this case study illustrated how these principles could grow a spiritual leadership and transform the congregations. In the Brazil case studies, the data suggests that while the same principles will continue to be successful, the focus must change from turnaround and renewal to accelerating and sustaining. This article shows how the Leadership Incubator is successful in a broad contextualization of the varied culture found in America; but in the international setting there is still much which needs to be learned. It may be possible that these same principles, if found scriptural, may also help within the declining leadership, found within the body of Christ.[38]

---

36   Rodney Stark, "Why Religious Movements Succeed or Fail: A Revised General Model." *Journal of Contemporary Religion*, (1996) 133-146.

37   Rochford and Bailey, *Almost Heaven,* 15.

38   Sims and Lopes, *Spiritual Leadership*, 59-86.

The article "Saints, Shepherds, Preachers, and Scholars: Leadership Crisis in the Churches of Christ," is actually a transcript from the November 25, 1991, annual Restoration Quarterly Breakfast. In it, John F. Wilson addresses the loss of true shepherding and preaching in the modern congregation as opposed to that of years gone by. Wilson addresses the way many preachers today only tolerate the elders as long as they leave them alone. He also addresses how that even the years of study and research are seen as irrelevant to most as it does not pertain to the heartfelt religion of the twenty-first century. The bright spot in this message is that there is still a faithful remnant that, regardless of the theology, anecdotal preaching, and "befuddled shepherding," remains true to the biblical call of God. If the leaders would get on with their responsibilities like the remnant, then there would be no "Leadership crisis in the churches of Christ."[39]

Summary

In summary, Chapter 2 examined and synthesized current literature on church leadership. It has documented the known biblical basis of leadership and shown that over the course of time there has been a change in how church leadership is viewed compared to the first century church. It even suggests that there is an identity crisis along with a crisis of leadership itself.[40] This information also shows the need to reevaluate how modern congregations view their elders and the procedures of preparing men for leadership positions. In Chapter 3, I will discuss the procedures and research methodology to be used in this research, the research subjects, the questions asked, how the data will be collected, and the procedures for analyzing that data.

---

39 John F. Wilson, "Saints, Shepherds, Preachers, and Scholars: Leadership Crisis in Churches of Christ," *Restoration Quarterly* 34, no. 3 (1991): 129-134.
40 Ibid., 129.

Chapter 3:

Methodology

This chapter will explain the methodology of the research used to evaluate the spiritual health and search for the factors leading to the absence of elders in the church. This research will be done from a qualitative nature. Leedy and Ormrod state that in qualitative studies the characteristics and qualities with all their nuances and complexities are observed.[1] I looked at the characteristics and qualities of the current leadership as seen by the membership of the nine congregations used for this study. This section will discuss how the research was obtained and evaluated, to understand the status of the eldership, as seen by those under their care.

I then evaluated what was known from past elderships by a case study and compared them to ascertain what has changed over the years. The first part of this study took place by mailing out surveys to the participants. After they had taken the survey, they took part in an oral interview. The congregation without elders that I selected for case study was chosen for the purpose of finding out if they have had elders in the past and what measures, if any, are being taken now to prepare men to be elders.

The data collected by this research showed the current knowledge and attitudes of those in the study presently regarding church leadership. It helped me to understand what steps can be taken, if any, to help prepare the next generation of elders. In Chapter 4, the data from the

---

1   Leedy and Ormrod, *Practical Research*, 251.

questionnaires and interviews will be presented. In Chapter 5, that data will be analyzed and presented in a holistic and cohesive manner.

Description of research design

Within the qualitative research design, I used the grounded theory method. Carl Auerbach and Louise Silverstein explain, "Grounded theory research allows the researcher to admit that he may not know enough to pose a specific question. In fact, he may not know what the right question is until he has finished collecting and analyzing the data. Therefore, instead of reading the literature for a specific question or problem, grounded theory instructs him to look for issues that are open and unclear. Research issues are found by looking for perspectives that are left out, and assumptions that need to be challenged."[2] I am using this type of research to find out the perspectives and assumptions which have been left out and have contributed to the change in church eldership. Leedy and Ormrod also state that the "theory that emerges from the study is derived from and rooted in data that has been collected in the field rather than taken from the research literature."[3] The need for the case study is based upon the need to know how the eldership of the twentieth-century self-replicated. Robert Yin says that "a case study allows investigators to focus on a 'case' and retain a holistic and real-world perspective – such as in studying individual life cycles, small group behavior, organizational and managerial processes, neighborhood change, school performance, international relations, and the maturation of industries."[4] Within these two studies, I have used surveys, interviews, and case studies of both past and present eldership models.

---

2   Carl F. Auerbach and Louise B. Silverstein, *Qualitative Data: An Introduction to Coding and Analysis* (New York, New York University Press, 2003), 14-15.

3   Leedy and Ormrod, *Practical Research*, 256.

4   Robert K. Yin, *Case Study Research, Design and Methods* (Los Angeles, Sage Publication Ltd. 2014), 4.

Sources and nature of the data

Participants in the Study

I had thirty participants for this study from nine different congregations—five from Texas and four from Oklahoma. They were made up of adults of various ages ranging from 32 to 84 years old and included both men and women. The only requirement was that they must be members of the church of Christ in either Texas or Oklahoma. These participants' perspectives of their elderships were valuable for this study as they showed the characteristics and the qualities of elders as they understood them to be. With many of the participants being above sixty, they also have a knowledge of the eldership qualities of the twentieth-century. The liberal or conservative status of the participant was not a consideration as to the criteria of their involvement because both types make up the various congregations and have an influence on the leadership obtained in those congregations.

Each of the thirty participants agreed to finish both the survey as well as the interview with the understanding that neither their identity nor the identity of the congregation in which they attend would ever be made known. It was explained to them that if they desired to drop out, all information obtained from them would be immediately discarded and not used. There was some hesitation on the part of some participants, because they did not want to be seen as a trouble maker. There were some who expressed a fear of retaliation on the part of elders if it became known they had taken part.

In the case study, two different congregations agreed to participate.[5] One has an eldership, one does not. Each agreed to set aside a time to discuss the various aspects used to develop future leadership. Those studied also discussed what has happened in the past making the eldership possible, or what caused them to lose their elderships. The requirement is that the congregation be a church of Christ and located in either Texas or Oklahoma.

---

5   The questions for the case study are found in Appendices C, D, E, and F.

Nature of Data

The three instruments used to obtain the data needed for this research are self-reported surveys, interviews with the participants, and intensive interviews with either elderships of congregations with elders or long-standing members of congregations that do not have elders.

In the first tool, the survey (Appendix B), the participants were given ten questions on which they rated their level of agreement concerning the various elements of their knowledge and attitude on the leadership of the church of Christ. I decided upon questions that I felt would give insight into their understanding of biblical principles as well as the character and quality of the elders in their congregations. The participants were given four possible answers based on the Likert scale of *"Highly Agree"* to *"Highly Disagree"* For example:

I believe Paul instructed all congregations to develop elders.
Highly Agree   Agree   Disagree   Highly Disagree

When the survey is broken down into its various parts, it has two questions for each area of concern in the eldership: study, need for elders, the authority of elders, mentoring of future elders, desire to be an elder. Because I did not know who would be taking part in the study, I wanted to make the survey as easy as possible. The survey sent out could be completed even without instruction. This kind of survey, according to Leedy and Ormrod, helps one to quantify people's behavior or attitudes.[6] It would also help me to understand the participants' attitude toward the current eldership.

The second tool, the interview that is used (Appendix C), was done one-on-one. A paper copy was sent out with the Informed Consent Form with the understanding that I would call and set up a time for this interview. It was left up to the participant as to whether it would be done in person or over the phone. Either way, it was recorded, or those recordings transcribed into a hard copy. The questions used were open ended questions, meant to give the participants the ability to answer as they

---

6   Leedy and Ormrod, *Practical Research*, 144.

understood the question. I wanted them to tell me what they thought about matters such as:

1. *How important they believed it was to have elders?*

2. *Is it important that elders mentor young men to be elders?*

3. *How important are the qualities of elders as mentioned in the Scriptures?*

4. *How much authority do elders have within the congregation?*

5. *When it comes to scriptural matters, is the preacher, or the elders, the main source of information?*

The questions from the interview helped me to determine what the congregations consider the elders' qualities and abilities in the church of Christ are today.

The third tool was the case study. With this study, I was trying to ascertain the holistic real-world perspective of the eldership in the twenty-first century to compare with the twentieth century. This is the strength of the case study as described by Yin.[7] By looking at congregations who have current elderships, and by finding out what steps they take to continue to have qualified men to replenish the eldership when needed, and then studying congregations which do not have elders, I hoped to find information needed to make it possible to replicate the elder training capabilities in all congregations of the churches of Christ.

This was accomplished by having interviews with elderships and groups of long time members of the various congregations. In these interviews, the discussions focused on how long these congregations had or have not had elders. If they do not have elders, I wanted to find out if they did in the past, and if they did, what took place that caused the loss

____

7   Yin, *Case Study Research*, 4. Yin states that "a case study allows investigators to focus on a 'case' and retain a holistic and real-world perspective."

of that eldership? The interviews included discussion about what steps are being taken to qualify men for the eldership in the future.

Criteria for the validity of data

In any research study, the question must be answered, "Does the study measure or describe what it is supposed to measure or describe?"[8] It must be done in such a way that the reader can have confidence that my conclusions are reasonable and that another researcher facing the same data would come to the same conclusion. In order to maintain that confidence, it was necessary to use triangulation, comparing and contrasting results from the multiple methods each described previously in this chapter. However, triangulation is not the cure all, seeing that even with multiple methods the interpretation is still limited to the context of those being studied. Tim Sensing explains, "Triangulation allows the researcher to substantiate the picture that is being seen and interpreted, but it is not the pot of gold at the end of the rainbow. Subsequently, the theory of triangulation and multi-methods is not a quick and easy substitute for the positivists' search for validity."[9]

For that reason, another validation is used to support the first. That validation is "Thick Description." Sensing says that "the more detailed analysis that you provide the reader, the more credible your work. When the reader can follow your analysis, your reliance on data and the paper trail you followed, your ethos as a researcher is enhanced for a detailed understanding of thick description."[10] If I make sure that the instrument used to assess my data measures the information that I intended it to measure then, according to Leedy and Ormrod, it can be considered as valid.[11]

---

8   Tim Sensing, *Qualitative Research; A Multi-Methods Approach to Projects for Doctor or Ministry Theses* (Eugene, Oregon, Wipf and Stock Publishers, 2011), 219.

9   Ibid., 220.

10   Ibid., 222.

11   Leedy and Ormrod, *Practical Research*, 96.

Collection of data

The qualitative data for this research project was collected in three phases. First, in my initial contact with the participants, I included the informed consent form, the church leadership survey, and the questions for the church leadership interview. They signed and completed the informed consent and answered the church leadership survey questions and returned them in the self-addressed envelope. Upon receiving them all I sat down and evaluated their answers to the survey. As part of the informed consent form the participants sent me a phone number with which to contact them. Using this number, I set up a time for collecting the second phase of data, the interview.

At the appointed time, I contacted each participant and we conducted the interview which took on the average twenty minutes. This conversation was recorded and then transcribed so that a hard copy could be kept and evaluated. This was all done on an individual basis, without anyone else in the room so it was all kept confidential. The transcribed data was then placed in the locked file cabinet in my office. During these interviews, I became an active listener. I was not there to give input, but rather to understand and examine the participants' answers to the questions. I tried to make the interview look the way that Leedy and Ormrod described, "as an informal conversation, with the participant doing most of the talking and the researcher doing most of the listening."[12]

After the qualitative data collection, I then began working on the case studies. Each of the congregations participating in the case study was contacted and a time to meet set up. During this meeting, there was a discussion on the design of the mentoring processes used to stimulate leadership growth within that congregation, how long they have had elders, or if they do not have elders, whether they ever had a leadership. If they at one time had elders and do not now, I wanted to know why not. Some of the congregations admitted that they do little to stimulate the maturity of elders, but let it "take a natural course."

---

12   Ibid., 256.

Qualitative data analysis

Using a grounded theory method of collecting data made it important for me to notice the patterns of words and phrases used by those being interviewed. Auerbach and Silverstein define a theory as "a description of a pattern that you find in the data."[13] The main purpose of the data collection was to identify and analyze these patterns. During the analysis of the transcripts, the main goal was to move from the raw text to the research concerns as it applies to the eldership of the church. In doing so I listened to what the subjects were saying as an active listener so that the concerns of the participant were what took center stage. Because the grounded theory deals with the overall process and spiritual growth of the eldership, the data included not just the actions of people, but also their feelings. During the interviews, the participants many times expressed the same ideas, often even using some of the same expressions. These patterns are referred to as repeating ideas.[14] It is these repeated ideas which are grouped together from the relevant data. This is considered to be the most difficult and labor-intensive portion of what these authors call the *coding process.*[15] In comparing these repeated ideas, I was able to organize them into a fuller picture of the current state of the eldership in the twenty-first century.

Linking data

There is a need for comparing the data from two groups of participants. First, there was the layperson, sitting in the pew. This constituted the group of thirty individuals who volunteered to participate in the survey and interview process. Then, there is the one group of elders and one group of church leaders (not elders) willing to participate in the case study. While the data collected dealt with the same topic, these groups were looking at the issues from different perspectives. During the analysis, there was a *constant comparative method* as I continually looked for

---

13   Auerback and Silverstein, *Qualitative Data,* 31.

14   Ibid., 53.

15   Ibid., 61.

the patterns which existed in data collected.[16] The desired outcome was to be able to link the data from both groups and ascertain the complete picture of the spiritual health in the eldership today compared to that of the twentieth century.

Summary

The design of this study is qualitative research. It consists of survey, interview, and case study. The first two were done with the members, as they view the eldership. The case study was done on the leading group of the church, discussing how they assess the spiritual health of the eldership both past and present. I analyzed the survey and interview transcripts, looking for the patterns and descriptive reflections. In the case study, I looked at patterns of spiritual growth in the leadership or the lack thereof as they were presented to me. Then, I presented them in a cohesive manner in Chapter 4. All of this assisted me in understanding the present condition of our elderships and how we came to be in our current status.

---

16   Leedy and Ormrod, Practical Research, 252. Here it is explained that "in qualitative research, however, the methodology often involves an iterative process in which the researcher moves back and forth between data collection and data analysis in what is sometimes called the *constant comparative method*." This took place as I looked for the patterns in the interviews as they were conducted.

Chapter 4

Presentation of Data

The purpose of this study was to look for some of the causes contributing to the decline seen in the leadership in churches of Christ in both Texas and Oklahoma. All data shown here was collected from thirty participants who are members of the church of Christ from these two states. There are a total of nine congregations represented here, five from Texas and four from Oklahoma. There is also data given from two case studies. One study was done with a congregation that has elders and one that does not. In this chapter I will present the data collected from the surveys, interviews, and the case studies as collected from the participants of this study. I am not speaking, in any way, concerning the church at large.

To use the survey for qualitative research I had to use it in such a way that it could be analyzed in percentages. The findings of the survey which was sent out to each participant are as follows. In this survey I asked questions that would address the four research questions found on pages 3 and 4. In doing so, I was able to ascertain in percentage form how the eldership is viewed by the laity. Following are the results of that survey taken by the 29 participants.

Church Leadership Survey

1. The congregation I attend encourages me to make time each day to study the Word of God.
   Highly Agree 70%   Agree 7%   Disagree 23%   Highly Disagree 0%

2. I believe a congregation with qualified men does not have to have an eldership to be pleasing to God.
   Highly Agree 7%   Agree 3%   Disagree 47%   Highly Disagree 43%

3. I believe Paul instructed all congregations to develop elders.
   Highly Agree 63%   Agree 30%   Disagree 0%   Highly Disagree 7%

4. I believe the eldership has biblical authority to make decisions for the local congregation.
   Highly Agree 73%   Agree 27%   Disagree 0%   Highly Disagree 0%

5. I believe elders today have as much biblical knowledge as those of the Twentieth Century.
   Highly Agree 10%   Agree 40%   Disagree 40%   Highly Disagree 10%

6. Elders I know spend time teaching young men how to be good elders.
   Highly Agree 7%   Agree 53%   Disagree 33%   Highly Disagree 3%

7. Elders today are held up in high esteem.
   Highly Agree 10%   Agree 70%   Disagree 20%   Highly Disagree 0%

8. I believe elders today have the ability and the desire to mentor the next generation of elders.
   Highly Agree 13%   Agree 57%   Disagree 30%   Highly Disagree 0%

9. Men today have a desire to become elders.
   Highly Agree 0%   Agree 37%   Disagree 50%   Highly Disagree 13%

10. Elders today are known for leading the congregation in its spiritual growth.
   Highly Agree 10%   Agree 50%   Disagree 33%   Highly Disagree 7%

In the above survey, each participant was given ten questions that pertain to the way they view the elder and his work today. By turning the answers into percentages, we have a qualitative look at the laity's understanding of the elder, his quality of person, ability and desire to mentor, along with how well he and his Bible knowledge affects his congregation in their spiritual growth. In the chart below the survey, and the interviews will be compared side-by-side and then assessed by the researcher in order to analyze the patterns and trends found in the answers of the participants.

Survey Questions	Survey Answers	Interview Observations	Researcher Observations
Do elders encourage you to study?	94% yes, 6% no	72% said the church is not as knowledgable today as in the past, 24% said it is, 4% were neutral	The laity today is not studying God's Word like it used to, therefore biblical knowledge is declining
Must congregations with qualified men have elders to be pleasing to God?	89% said yes, only 9% said they did not think so	97% of interviewees agreed that having elders is important, while 3% were neutral	Of the 9 congregations represented in the study, 4 were without elders (and had been without for >10 years). 11 of the 29 interviewees were without elders
Are all congregations supposed to develop elders?	93% said yes, 7% said it was not important	38% did not observe the mentoring or teaching of future elders, 55% said they saw the desire in their elders to mentor, 7% were neutral	While 96% interviewed saw the need to mentor the next generation, only 2 of the 9 congregations represented had a program in place to train elders
Do elders have authority to make decisions for the local congregation?	100% said yes	59% thought the authority extended to the personal life of the laity, 31% said it only applied in matters of the congregation, 10% were neutral	31% took the position that elders dealt with problems at the building but not with an individual's life. Those who were neutral tended to lean toward that position.

Survey Questions	Survey Answers	Interview Observations	Researcher Observations
Is the biblical knowledge of the eldership as great as it was in the last century?	50% said yes, 50% said no	59% did not think today's elders have the ability to teach and defend the Word of God as those in the past. 31% said their knowledge is comparable. 10% did not answer.	93% saw the need for elders to be able to teach and defend the truth as a primary cause for the weakness of the church today, yet 82% said when spiritual questions arise they approach the preacher rather than the elders
Do today's elders mentor young men to be good elders?	60% said elders they know do mentor, 40% said no	55% said they saw a desire in elders to mentor. 7% said they did not know if the elders desired to mentor. 38% said elders do not desire to mentor.	Only 2 congregations reported having any type of formal mentoring or teaching in place. It was also reported that some of the congregations (not represented) had applicable programs such as Lads to Leaders.
Are today's elders respected and loved?	80% of those surveyed said yes, 20% said no	During interviews, 52% said they are not respected as they were in the past, 28% said they are. 20% were unsure.	Nearly all interviewees stated it depends on the elder's efforts. If the elder does a good job/is seen as a spiritual man, then they are respected. If he does a poor job/ doesn't lead, then they are not. Which means 52% do not believe today's elder does his job.
Do elders today have the ability and desire to mentor the next generation of elders?	69% said yes, 31% said no	During interviews, 55% said there was a desire and ability, 38% said no, 7% were neutral	Most interviewees said this is done through class and leading by example. Only 2 congregations had formal programs in place.
Do men today desire to be elders?	63% said no, 37% said yes	It should be noted that the most difficult qualification to find is the desire for the office. Interviewees attributed this to the observation of abuse taken by current elders.	One of the main reasons discovered for a congregation not having elders has proven to be a lack of desire. The case study showed that of 600 members, during the last elder selection only 2 men possessed the attributes and desire.

Survey Questions	Survey Answers	Interview Observations	Researcher Observations
Do elders today lead congregations in spiritual growth?	60% agreed. 40% disagreed. When asked during interviews about the discrepancy between survey and interview answers, it was noted this is the way the laity thought Biblical elders should be seen, as shepherds.	During interviews, only 45% reported observing their elders in their work as shepherds, feeding and leading the flock. 55% viewed their elders as administrators.	The failure of shepherds to lead congregations is the reason for many of the failures in local congregations. When elderships act as administrators, the congregation usually has a disdain for the elder and a lack of spiritual growth is seen. In addition, a lack of numerical growth seems to follow.

Interviews

In order to present the data collected in the interviews I will present it looking at six different categories as the participants viewed them. These categories are: 1) The View of Current Elders' Oversight, 2) The Importance of Elderships in the Local Congregations, 3) Spiritual Maturity of the Church, 4) The Mentoring of the Next Generation of Elders, 5) Qualities of the Shepherds, and 6) Communication of the Elders. These categories were derived from the information that the questions addressed. For example, when asked if the elders are seen as administrators or shepherds, the answers describe how the elders are viewed in their job. Each category will be addressed individually to avoid confusion. During this section, a code was used to identify the interview from which the quotes are coming. Each time the quote is given, the interview will be noted by the abbreviation INT. followed by the number of that interview. The interview demographics can be found in Appendix H.

The view of current elders' oversight

The question was asked, "The elders today, how do you view these elders?" Almost 45% of those interviewed saw the elders as doing the job of a shepherd. Also from the interviews there were sixteen out of twenty-nine that saw them as administrators. That is, 55.1% of the participants see today's elders as administrators, while all the participants agree that they should be shepherds instead.[1] It was also stated that it is thought that most do not know how to shepherd. One participant said, "My experience has been both. I think the current elders seem to be more administrators because they don't know how to shepherd."[2] It seems that there is a connection between these administrators and micromanaging. One participant even went as far to say, "What I'm seeing around here that I can actually speak to, I see a little micromanagement, instead of leading and guiding. It's more of just putting people where they want them to be."[3]

There was 55.1% seeing the elders as administrators. That left 44.8% who viewed them as shepherds. Most of these viewed them based upon their current elders. One of the participants stated that, "I want to answer two-fold in that where I came from four years ago you know it was very much administrator and where I am now is very much shepherding."[4] Several of the participants who view them as shepherds do so based upon the local congregation they attend and admitted having little to no interaction with any other elderships.[5] One of the participants seemed to state a popular view of the elders when he said, "Well many of the elders of today are, in fact, administrators rather than shepherds. But the biblical image of the elder was to be a shepherd therefore leading

---

1   Appendix I. All of the percentages found in the interview are located in Appendix I.

2   INT. 13.

3   INT. 11.

4   INT. 14.

5   INT. 14, 15, 12, 19, 24.

and caring for the church rather than administering the actual physical parts of the church."[6] This participant does a great deal of traveling and has close ties to many congregations found in the states of Oklahoma, Texas, New Mexico, and Colorado. He was making this statement in accordance with his own experience. However, this sentiment was expressed by several participants.

Another aspect in the view of the elders is the amount of respect, love, and affections that these men receive from their congregations. Of those interviewed 51.7% stated that today's elders do not receive the respect and love of those in times past, 34.4% said that that the elder does, while 13.7% says it is about the same. It was stated by both those who do not see the same respect as well as those that do, that respect is given to the elders because of the work they do. One participant stated, "Many times that respect or appreciation has gone to the local minister or the local preacher rather than the elders because the elders were not doing what they should and again if they were doing what they were supposed to do they would have received respect. But because they were not, they were not receiving that appreciation."[7] It is also pointed out that the man who is faithful and more active and able to make decisions based upon God's Word will have the love and respect of those who he leads.[8]

The data also states that society does not show respect to authority, as it did just a century ago. One participant stated, "I have to assume no because in general society, as a whole, does not show much respect for authority of any kind. So, I would think that has to filter into the church also."[9] One participant even points to the fact that the world's lack of respect can be seen in the dress and lack of modesty, the disrespect for the laws of the land, and even a lack of respect for the office of President, our flag and our nation. This participant stated, "I do not believe there is a lot of respect in this world today. When you see some of these women in the world that are dressed the way they are, they do not respect themselves or anybody else. When you see people driving down the

---

6   INT. 4.

7   INT. 3.

8   INT. 7. Also look at interviews 9, 13, 25, 28.

9   INT. 5.

highway they do not respect the law. This recent mess with sports and the President they do not respect authority. There is a lack of respect in this world overall and in every corner from what it was a century ago."[10] It is suggested by one participant that this lack of respect is showing the failure of both the home and the church. Another participant said, "We're not teaching people to respect even God let alone elders or the flag or anybody else."[11]

There is also found within the data that this lack of respect cultivates within the men who should be future elders a lack of desire. Knowing that the job of shepherding the flock is one with little or no respect and appreciation, qualified men lose the desire to become elders. They refuse a job in which a headache and heartache are all that is seen. For example, in interview 8 the participant was asked the question, "Do elders receive the respect, love, and affection that the elders in times past received?" The interviewee stated, "Absolutely not! One of the reasons we do not have elders here is because of the backbiting and back stabbing that's talked about in Galatians the 5th chapter. So, the men do not desire the office. I've got men that are qualified right here, right now. The only reason they're not doing the work is the lack of desire."[12]

Another thought expressed in the data is that education might be one of the reasons for the lack of respect. We have a generation that has a much higher graduate level of education compared to a generation ago. And when the older, less secular educated person becomes an elder, the younger generation does not recognize the difference in Bible learning and higher education. One participant stated, "I think it's because of the educational level of the younger people that are saying well I'm just as smart as they are. While they do not realize they may be able to do quantum physics, they are not able to teach and understand the Bible due to a lack of Bible knowledge. And that's the difference between years past like in the 50's and 60's as compared to now."[13]

---

10   INT. 29.

11   INT. 28.

12   INT. 8.

13   INT. 23.

It must also be pointed out that when looking at the respect that elders receive, 13.7% of the participants claim that elders receive the same as in times past. All four of these participants equate the respect received with the kind of job the elder is doing. If the elder is truly qualified and doing the job of a shepherd, then he receives the love and respect of the congregation. If he is not doing the work, then he finds himself being despised and rejected in his position. Another participant, on the issue of love and respect stated it the clearest when he said, "You know (how much love and respect the elder receives) that depends on how they shepherd. I mean some do and some don't. You know, I hate to say the good ones, but a good elder will get the respect.... on the other side of that is, if you're just a complaint department and a fire stomper then you're going to have problems."[14]

The Importance of Elderships in the Local Congregations

When asked the question, "How important is it for the local congregation to have elders?" twenty-eight out of twenty-nine said extremely important.[15] Twelve out of twenty-nine participants even state that it is biblical. That is 41.3%. The best answer here is interview 5 stating, "Well I believe it is commanded biblically to have elders. I believe it is God's will, so it is important. If we want to follow God's will, then we would have elders."[16] The one who did not hold it extremely important had a neutral attitude. He stated, "I have been in situations where it's both and I believe that elders are the better of the two."[17] While he had rather have elders, he just sees it as the better of the two options. The data collected also showed an interesting trend, that out of the nine congregations represented four do not have elderships. And out of twenty-nine people interviewed eleven worshipped where there are no elders. Yet, all but one sees it as extremely important.

---

14   INT. 13. Refer also to Interviews 3, 7, 9.

15   Appendix I

16   INT. 5.

17   INT. 17.

When asked what effect not having elders had on the congregation there were four main reasons given. First is the point that not having elders allows a lack of biblical teaching and for error to enter into the congregation. 37.9% of those interviewed would reference this as one of the main reasons for the importance of having elders. In fact, the very first interview states, "It leaves room for error and false teaching, and a lack of learning about those things."[18]

The second reason given is that a congregation without elders becomes stunted, or dies all together. One participant stated, "It is extremely important to have good spiritual elders in the local congregation, if in fact that local congregation will not only survive but grow."[19] Later the same participant says, "It stunts the growth of a congregation not to have good leading people. And it is probably the greatest problem in the church today, is not having qualified leaders, elders within the congregations."[20]

A third reason given for not having solid eldership is that of either having chaos or a very slow acting congregation in its decision-making process. Looking at interview 5, the statement is made in answer to the question is "well there is chaos and confusion."[21] When there is no authority available the data shows that the process of making decisions and protecting the flock from false teaching becomes anyone's game. Participant 16 is recorded as saying "…you don't have the knowledge base there, so you can make decisions based on God's Scripture that He gave us… I just think a lot of emotions get involved in those things, and a lot of opinions, a lot of personal beliefs and it's just not the way God intended."[22] Another participant, who has no elders and works off men's

---

18 INT. 1. "Those things" was in reference to the importance of having qualified shepherds within the congregation. Also reference interviews 2, 6, 12, 13, 15, 18, 19, 24, 25 on this point of error and lack of teaching.

19 INT. 4.

20 Ibid. See also interviews 6, 22, 26, and 28.

21 INT. 5.

22 INT. 16.

business meetings, said "You end up with men's meetings and you get about 50% less done by not having elders in my experience."[23]

The fourth issue with not having elderships is that of the congregation falling into the denominational style of leadership of the "Pastoral System." When there is no eldership to look up to the preacher is the next in the line of leadership. This is a point that will be addressed in greater detail later in the data. But, here under this topic one participant stated, "I am aware of some congregations who have tried to have unqualified elders, or having men that do not meet the qualifications because they were looking to have leaders. They were looking for administrators instead of shepherds. Many of them were looking to the minister or preacher to take care of that."[24]

Spiritual Maturity of the Church

One aspect of church leadership is the feeding and oversight of the Lord's church. In the interview process the data showed that 93.1% of the participants saw a direct correlation with the elder's ability to teach and preach and the spiritual maturity of the congregation. That is twenty-seven out of twenty-nine participants. Yet, only 31.6% of the participants saw the abilities of the current elders to teach and train to be on par with those of the 60's and 70's. The data showed 58.6% saw the elders as being inadequate of truly teaching those that they would hope to lead. One participant stated how that in the 60's the elders were men who were obviously God fearing, God believing, leaders wanting to do what was right according to God's word and showed it in their action. They lived the life of Matthew 6:33 having God first and foremost in their thoughts. He then said, "The men that are elders today do not seem to be ready to demonstrate their belief in God, their desire of making the church grow... What we see today is, 'well kind of'."[25] Along this line the data shows that 72.1% of those interviewed do not see the church today as spiritually mature as it was in the twentieth century. They based

---

23   INT. 27. Also reference interviews 8, 9, 10, 11, 14, 16, 19, 20, and 21.

24   INT. 3.

25   INT. 4.

their observation on the biblical knowledge possessed by the majority of the members. One participant said, "In times before the church was known as walking Bibles. They were known as people that spoke where the Bible spoke and were silent where the Bible was silent, but more importantly the members of the Lord's church were known as a people that knew their Bibles inside out, upside down, backwards and forwards. And Mike, I don't know about you and where you're at, but that's something that is not true where I'm at anymore."[26] Another stated that "we are not as spiritually minded as a congregation, we're not as biblically literate as we were even when I became a Christian which was 35 years ago."[27]

The data, which shows the 93.1% agreeing that there is a correlation between the elder's ability to teach and preach with the spiritual maturity of the church, was summed up in a single statement, "No congregation rises above its leadership and so if you have elders who are not sharing their faith then you're probably not going to have a congregation sharing their faith. And if they are not teaching the congregation's not going to be teaching. They have got to set the pace."[28]

Participants also showed a concern that by elders setting the example of not teaching and preaching then there becomes a reliance upon the preacher. And when this happens it becomes easier for error to enter in.[29] This also sets up the data collected on who, within the congregation addresses scriptural matters. The data showed that 82% of the participants stated that the preacher was the one who most often is approached to answer scriptural matters. Many of the participants see this to be the cause for two reasons. "First, because it is a paid position, and secondly because they are better educated in biblical matters."[30] Another participant said, "They get up in front of us every week and they are grounded in the scripture and we hear them more than we hear the elders, so we

---

26   INT. 8.

27   INT. 21.

28   INT. 21.

29   INT. 10.

30   INT. 5. See also interviews 2, 8, 9, and 13.

assume that they are you know more grounded in or have the scripture readily available."[31]

The Mentoring of the Next Generation of Elders

The data collected on the mentoring process was mixed with 55.1% believing that the current eldership had a desire to mentor the next generation of elders and 37.9% reporting they did not see a desire within the congregations they had any interaction with. While only 6.8% (2 participants) were neutral - not knowing whether or not the elders today had any desire to mentor. When it came to the importance of mentoring, 96.5% said it was extremely important. Most took the same stance in that they felt it was of extreme importance because "of the age of elders, they are not going to be able to work for a long period of time and they need to be training and mentoring younger men and instilling in them the desire to serve as elders."[32] One participant even stated how that elders should be working themselves out of a job, "I personally believe elders should be replicating themselves. They should be helping train up that next generation so that when they have stepped down because of physical infirmities and the aging process, there will be a group of men who are already in place to help the church excel more in the next generation than it did in the last one."[33] Those who see the desire present also see that it is being done by different methods of mentoring. While 20% of that number sees it being done by the example which is set by the existing elders (Interviews 6, 15, 19, 21), another 25% report that mentoring is being done by the teaching of the Word of God (Interviews 2, 8, 11, 14, 16). Then 15% say it is done by replication leading of the younger men. This would be the actual taking them by the hand and showing them step by step the work of the elder (Interviews 3, 11, 26). And 40% report it being done by special classes and programs such as Lads to Leaders (Interviews 12, 20, 28, 1, 17, 18, 22, 23).

------

31   INT. 17.

32   INT. 3. Also see interviews 5, 8, and 27.

33   INT. 29.

When asked the question of how do you see or not see the mentoring process being done, thirteen reported that they were not seeing it done at all. That is 44.8% of the participants interviewed. And they had some very specific reasons which they saw as the problem. Almost 69% of that number stated that the current eldership just did not take action. While many want to mentor, many lack the knowledge or just never started the process (interviews 4, 7, 13, 16, 21, 24, 25, 27, and 28). Three participants (23%) said that it's because there were not any elders so there could not be any mentoring (Interviews 8, 9, and 10).

Qualities of the Shepherds

When discussing the qualities or attributes of elders, 100% of the data showed that the attributes shown in 1 Timothy 3:1-7 and Titus 1:6-9 are essential to the elder being able to do his work as God would have him to. One participant when asked the question of how important those attributes are said, "Absolutely imperative, he can be a scriptural elder only by meeting those qualifications."[34] Another interviewee stated that "they are incredibly important it's kind of the whole point. You know those qualifications weren't just thrown in there as you know a good guideline. They were rules they were the qualifications that they must meet to be one of God's elders."[35] Many of the interviews would show that because of the importance of the attributes we must teach them to the young men early so they will aspire to fulfill the attributes. One participant stated it like this, "I think they are very important. I think that first of all that an individual needs to aspire to or want to serve as

---

34   INT. 8. Unfortunately, within his answer he also states that he feels that one of the problems and why we don't have elders is because we are trying to put perfect men in the job and there are no perfect men. This is a problem, not that there are no perfect men, but that they would feel the attributes are extremely important but are willing to compromise these attributes because there are only a few qualified men.

35   INT. 16. He also points out that part of the problem is the fact that these attributes are being bent and slanted to our own interpretations instead of staying true to the Word. And by doing so we have installed men into the office of elder who are not qualified.

an elder. And therefore, he will want to try to fulfill all of those qualifications, or attributes."[36]

While looking at the quality of the elder, the question of his authority was considered. When looking at the elder's responsibility to shepherd the flock, how far does his authority go? Does it stop at the church building? Does he only have the right to make corporate decisions or does he have the authority to enter into the private life of those he leads? 58.6 % stated that he had the biblical authority to watch over the flock in all of their spiritual life. That would include their private life if it were a matter of spiritual things. However, while this is the biblical stance it was recorded that many today will not yield to that authority, "I believe the elders that I know of today have biblical authority. However, the church is not as willing to submit to that authority as it was, I believe, in times past. And that's where I think we kind of missed that. That is what's going on here. Biblical authority has not changed. But the church's acceptance of that authority has changed. And young people don't submit the way they should."[37] In interview 29 the participant asserted that, "Because there is no respect for law, or for self, or for anybody else it is only natural that there remains no respect for the elders." The data collected also shows that 41.3% interviewed do not see the elders having the authority that God intended. Even if they are recognized as having authority, some see them not using what God has given them. Interviewee 25 states "I don't see them using the authority. I don't see them using what they're taught in the Bible to use. They just have their meetings and they don't get out and visit and teach and do like those we used to have."[38] The problem of authority I think can be found when the question is asked what is the elders' authority based upon? While 68.9% of those interviewed said it was based on the Bible, 31% still think the authority of elders is based upon what pleases them. One participant said, "It should be based on exactly what the Word of God says… unfortunately what is in practice is probably closer to the elder has authority to do whatever they feel they need to do for the church as

---

36   INT. 3.

37   INT. 4.

38   INT. 25.

long as it doesn't make me too uncomfortable or cross up what I want to do."[39] Unfortunately, this seems to be the mindset of not only members but also of some elders.

When asked about problems in the church the question was asked, "Who handles the problems that arise in the congregations?" 48.2% said the elders, 17.2% said the men of the congregation (most of these did not have elders) and 34.4% said the preacher. Unfortunately, most of the 34.4% do have elders and yet they prefer a pastoral type of setting. The reasons they sited is because of the preacher's relationship with the congregation, his paid position, and his advanced education of the Bible. Participant five answered this question by saying, "Overall the preacher is called on more than the elders. Not in every situation, but if I averaged it out it would be." When asked why he stated so he replied, "Multiple reasons. One: because of the carryover from denominational views of pastors and their complete control over the congregations. But also, just because the preachers are seen more. They are in the pulpit. They are available in the office. They are more easily accessible. And maybe because the elders have let it happen."[40]

Communication of the eldership

While reading any one of a dozen books on leadership success, one will find that one of the main sources for success is proper communication between the leaders and those he wishes to lead. In the interview there was one question designed specifically to gage the communication between the elders and the congregation. The question was asked how often do your elders meet? Out of the twenty-nine participants nineteen had elders. The answers are frightening. 63.1% of the participants, twelve out of nineteen did not know when their elders meet. The 36.8% (7) that did know were either elders, deacons, or preachers. Even the elders' wives did not know the answer to the question. Most simply said, "I have no idea."[41] This same participant also stated on the question of

------

39   INT. 29.

40   INT. 5.

41   INT. 5.

how was mentoring not being done answered that there was a lack of communication from the elders.

Case study with elders

The case study of the large congregation with elders was conducted on a Saturday morning with five of the ten elders of a congregation that is between a 110 and 112 years old. They have had an eldership for over 100 years without ever having a gap in leadership. When asked how they viewed the work of the elders, as shepherds or administrators, the answer was immediate and unanimous, "*Shepherds!*" Then they explained that they did not want to be administrators, and that the Bible did not afford them the luxury of being administrators.

When asked if they as a group saw a shortage of elders in the church today, they answered one at a time, "Yes." Being a large congregation, many smaller congregations come to them for help. Over the course of time they have been approached more and more by congregations without elders. Also, as they travel from place to place they have seen the decline. When asked, "What do you see as the cause of the shortage of elders?" they opened up one at a time and recounted what they had seen both within the local congregation and in their traveling as they visited other congregations. They said they had noticed that there was a group of men between the ages of fifty and up that has lost the commitment to serving the church. They had noticed in the younger men a new commitment to serve but they did not know how to accomplish the task. Because of this lack of knowledge, there is a lot of past history problems, where they have done things that prevent them from being an elder. This younger group also are so focused on family and careers that they don't have the time to devote to be an elder. But, the main cause for the shortage that they have noticed is the lack of desire to serve. This seems to correlate across the age groups. They also stated that the present elders in many cases are not necessarily trying to develop others to replace themselves when the time comes. They attributed this to a lack of vision on the part of the congregation and the need to develop that next group of leaders.

So, many of the elderships in the churches of Christ are not willing to replicate self. On the other hand, these elders are not seeing men willing to step up to the plate (for the reasons mentioned above) and be responsible as elders either. It was stated during the interview that, "Some now are so focused on family and careers that they do not have time to devote to be an elder."[42] These younger men are willing to serve in other areas, but they don't want to move into the direction of becoming elders. One of the participants stated, "We are not seeing men willing to step up to the plate in responsibility in the area of eldership. They are willing to serve and to work in different areas, but not in the direction of being an elder."[43] The example was given of their local work. How they were looking to add more elders and went to everyone they could come up with that had the attributes found in the Bible. One 600+ congregation was only able to find two names that were qualified. It was stated that there were many who they talked to that qualified in every area except they did not desire the work.

The question was asked, "If there was a plan to replicate the elders here?" The answer was that there was an unwritten desire to bring on new elders. The elders make it a point to encourage men who have the attributes to work toward the time when they would become elders. This group of elders has initiated a program where they not only talk to the men whom they feel are qualified; but they encourage them to begin getting ready for that transition in the future. Then the elders begin trying to mentor them to think about and head them in the direction of becoming an elder. This is an area that these elders have increased their efforts in the near past as opposed to the lack of effort they had made. This is not to say that they did not do it in the past, just that it may not have been as purposefully engaged in as it is now.

The follow-up question for this discussion is, "Other than talk, what else is being done to ensure that there's not a shortage of elders here in the future?" One of the elders commented, "I was just thinking the same thing. We talk, it's mentioned, and it's discussed a lot but there's not a formal class that's set up for elder development and that's

---

42   Case Study Large Congregation.

43   Ibid.

something that's probably worth talking about and thinking about and working on more."[44] It was mentioned that they do discuss a lot with the ministers, the developing of the young people, but maybe it is time to think about setting up and working on elder development. They see the need for more preaching and teaching on living your life correctly to reduce foolish mistakes which disqualify the man before he gets to that point in life.

Another aspect of this question is the mentoring process that they already employ. This group of elders when they are out visiting and doing things of that nature (where there is not a hush factor) try to take younger men along so that they learn that part of being a shepherd. They try to involve deacons in activities like visiting with missionaries and things of that nature and try to give them jobs which require responsibilities and the delegation of authority. This is done in order to help them take and get used to having responsibilities in spiritual areas.

Another program that this eldership does is at least once a year they meet with the 8th graders. They have a dinner with them and pray with them before they enter High School. They do the same thing with the seniors that are going out. They spend time with them letting them know who we are and a little bit more about what we are. During this time of the year they have several lessons on how the attributes of the shepherd are not just for them, but for every Christian. This is the same type of approach used when they start surveying for new elders. They help the members to understand that if they want to nominate someone, first, they must go to them and see if the desire is there and if there is anything else that may disqualify them. During this time the elders begin their own canvassing to see who they feel like may qualify and they begin putting together a possible list of future elders to work with.

New members are also an area that the elders here look at. The elders watch to see how involved they are and are willing to be. If they become involved the elders start looking at them after a given time to see how they would fill the deacon's and elder's role. Along that same line when someone wants to place membership, they have them come in on Sunday afternoon and visit with the elders that are at the building from

____

44   Ibid.

3:30 am—5:00 pm and discuss their past and their present and what they want to do to be involved. That helps the elders to know more about the people that are coming on board. They also have an involvement sheet to help show their gifts and work areas.

These initial talks help the elders to identify future elders who may not be completely qualified now but are still able to grow into the job, and help them to mature so that in the future they can serve as elders. Most of the mentoring is not done in formal classes as such but by spending a lot of one-on-one time with the person and leading them in the way they should go. It is also thought that the intensive Bible studies that are done within the congregation there are very important. The attendance of these Bible classes is not only expected but required for anyone who is to be considered as a future elder. That includes his family. As part of the mentoring process these individuals are asked specifically, "Will you do this" and give them assignments such as visiting or whatever for a specific length of time as part of their development. During this time the elder who is mentoring will spend time during the specific period talking with them and helping them perform the task better and many times the individual does not even realize they are mentoring him.

The next question dealt with the loss of eldership oversight compared to the 20th Century. While they have been able to maintain a sound eldership oversight in the local congregation they have noticed a loss in the brotherhood at large. As an example of why we are seeing this loss they used the influence of the culture around us. It was stated that, "Today many elders are not strong enough to stand on the Bible when the congregation wants to bring things in. They are not strong enough to say no we are going to stay with the Bible and not what the world wants to bring in."[45] If the eldership is to remain strong, then they must keep with the Bible teachings and not with what the world wants to do.[46]

There is data that supports that part of the problem that we have become a pastoral church.[47] The preacher has become the pastor of

---

45   Ibid.

46   Ibid.

47   Ibid.

the local church. The eldership sort of follows along and so goes the preacher so goes the church. In the surrounding congregations these weak elderships are based upon a lack of knowledge from God's Word and a lack of backbone to stand upon God's Word. In the congregation participating in the case study, which has sustained an eldership for over 100 years, it is just the opposite. They have maintained the scriptural plan of church leadership. The eldership influences the congregation and the ministers preach the doctrine of God with the backing of that eldership. Too many of the congregations, as reported by this eldership, are congregations that just go along with popular opinions. Too many congregations float here and float there, just wherever the congregation wants to go just to keep memberships. The elders said, "It is more of an entertainment world today, instead of a spiritual world. The congregations say, 'yeah we think we ought to have instrumental music because it will bring more people in the congregation.' Basically, they say this is what I like and not what God says."[48] Many of the congregations are becoming entertainment oriented rather than spiritually oriented. That is the reason for instrumental music and other programs to entertain the masses. The leaders of such congregations seem to "just get beaten down and give in."[49] In other congregations the culprit is not being scriptural to begin with. This type of elder gives into the, "Concept that it cannot hurt, or the Bible does not tell us not to. So, it takes a strong eldership to be able to look beyond the here and now to where these new devices will lead and that is what we have to look at all the time.[50]

While looking at what has been lost in the eldership, the answer comes out very strong that these elderships have lost a reverence for God's word. When asked, "What has been lost in the eldership today?" the participants stated, "The respect of the Word of God. Without the reverence for God's word then the pattern He has given us to follow is lost. The elders stated that when you look at the roll there you will see that they have gained many, "Members from other congregations because of the weak leadership and they came there looking for strong

---

48 Ibid.

49 Ibid.

50 Ibid.

leadership."[51] But it was warned that you will also see families lost because they would not yield to strong leadership. It was stated, "we have lost members because of a strong eldership because they are not willing to go along with what we see as scriptural."[52] It must be remembered that a biblical eldership cannot, and will not, go along with the desires of the congregation which are contrary to God's Word. The elders in this study have the desire to project a leadership in the principles of the Bible. As they are mentoring, directing, guiding, and shepherding they do so within the confines of the Bible. They see that as being their responsibility and that is what they intend to do. They stated it like this, "We can project a leadership in the principles of the Bible. That is mentoring, that is directing, that is guiding, that is shepherding, that is molding that is directing in God's path, that is what all of our (the elders) responsibility is, and that is what we are doing."[53]

Next, they were asked about the importance of communication with the congregation. This group of elders sees this as a vital part of the leadership role. And while they do it well they are always looking for ways of improving. In doing so they claim they have made some strides in opening the communication channels with the congregation but find that it is not always easy. It was stated, "We have tried to make some strides in finding ways to open with the congregation in areas where it matters, and they need to understand but that is not always easy."[54] They said, "It is easier to keep quiet, you know, but then you leave them out of things which they really need to know. That lets them know that you are being upfront and honest about what is going on."[55] To do that they have implemented a few things such as the service starts off with shepherd leading and it ends with a shepherd saying a prayer. This helps keep them visible. They also let the people know that there are elders available for them every Sunday afternoon from 3:30-5:00 pm. They try to express that the lines of communications are always open if they need

---

51   Ibid.

52   Ibid.

53   Ibid.

54   Ibid.

55   Ibid.

them. It was also recalled that regardless how hard they try to communicate, they inevitably will sit there and discuss the issues, and then leave, forgetting to officially make a point to pass on the information. But in trying to be available they have their phone numbers printed on the front page of the bulletin so that they are always in touch.

When looking at the spiritual level of the congregation there the elders consider it very strong compared to others in the surrounding areas. Most of the information on the spiritual strength of the congregation they claim is from feedback from other congregations. While it is hard to measure or compare, those who visit seem to sing their praises and remark on how mission oriented this congregation is. The older elders in this study are able to compare it to the same congregation from twenty years ago. And while the church was strong then, they see it as getting stronger all the time.

Considering the topic of men's business meetings, the general consensus is that there is not a need for it. If there was not a set of elders then there might be, but with elders there is no need. With an eldership, the elders meet and decide the issues then pass that information on. In this congregation they will meet, then meet with the deacons, and then it is passed to the congregation. It was suggested by one of the elders that if all the elders are active teachers they receive a lot of feedback from the congregation. Then with the meetings with the deacons they have more feedback with which they can make the necessary decisions and then communicate that back to the congregation.

In order to edify the congregation, having a good feel for the needs of the congregation because of the relationship with them, they are able to address issues in the class settings. In this way they are able to shut down many problems before they become real problems. For an example, on the congregational Facebook account someone posted something on the site which was a little extreme and someone else responded back in a very negative way. The elders took immediate action and got it resolved so that it could not grow. Then they teach how they are to respect and respond to the individual. All of their classes are designed as a discussion format which helps the congregation to gel as one family.

In conclusion to the study this eldership wanted to state that one of their biggest challenges, something that they have always had, is how to get more people to come to Bible class, how to get more people to come on Sunday nights and Wednesday nights. It is a never-ending battle. One elder summed up his thoughts with this paragraph:

> *"Mike, I believe that most elderships, I can't speak for all, but just most that I know about have moved away from the job, the task, and the responsibility that I believe the good book tells us. Some of what was done because of just a lack of knowledge and knowing what the responsibility was. Some of it was because of laziness. It's easier to let somebody else do it. I have known this congregation, for a while. Several years ago, the mentality was, well the elders should be in the background not in the front. And they, we have, this eldership has put a lot of effort, and continues to do so, to take back the responsibility of serving as elders, shepherding the flock, and move away from administrative responsibilities as much as we can. We have a good group of deacons. We still struggle with taking a hold of something instead of pushing it over to them. We are getting better at that. But just to remove the preacher from the pastor position and take our pastoral role as elders back is hard. I really believe that stand cause one individual to turn and walk away from this table one day because it was not something that he bought into and that was a preacher. He felt that the preacher should be the quarterback and the leader. I think after sitting and listening to this group for a little bit he saw pretty clearly that a preacher wasn't going to run the congregation here. But we worked real hard to try to reestablish the elder's role, the shepherd's role, and fulfill that responsibility as best we can."[56]*

In the case studies, I wanted to see the difference in what elders saw as needed skills in both establishing relationships, as well as in the task

---

56   Ibid.

oriented needs, and compare them to men without elderships. To assess these patterns, I gave the *Relational and Task Skills Survey (pages 68-69)* to all the elders who participated in the case study as well as all the men who participated from the congregation without elders. Then looked at the patterns of what they saw as needed or not needed. The other two inventory lists are found at the end of the case study without elders.

Case Study Congregation No Elders

This case study took place with a congregation that at one time had an eldership with an average attendance of eighty people. It now has not had elders for fifteen years and they now average thirty-five in attendance. When asked about the circumstance of losing their eldership, they said that the last eldership consisted of three men. One became ill and passed away leaving two. Then in just a short time another passed, and the eldership was dissolved. When asked if the congregation desired to have elders, "I hope so" was the reply. They were then asked, "Why do you desire to have elders?" The response was "I believe it's pleasing to God. I believe it's the way He intended the church to be."[57] They were then asked if they had noticed in their travels a decline in eldership oversight? And the answer was yes. The answer was being based on questions of congregations which had been visited as they traveled though Oklahoma and Texas. They had a desire to know the state of the church where they were going and asked questions.

They were then asked about the work of the elder. "How do you view the work of an elder as a shepherd or an administrator?" The reply was a shepherd. They were then asked, "If there any place for the elders to perform the role of an administrator?" After having to define administrator as a CEO type for them, they answered no. One of the participants stated, "If the eldership was truly acting as shepherds there was no room for the addition of the administrator."[58] Then it was asked if it was scriptural for a congregation not to have elders? They asked for an ex-

----

57   Case Study Congregation No Elders.
58   Ibid.

Relational Skills Inventory

Skill	necessity	needed	not needed	neutral
1. Listening	80%	20%	none	none
2. Networking	20%	80%	none	none
3. Conflict Resolution	80%	80%	none	none
4. Decision Making	100%	none	none	none
5. Risk Taking	60%	40%	none	none
6. Problem Solving	80%	20%	none	none
7. Confronting	60%	40%	none	none
8. Encouraging	80%	20%	none	none
9. Trust Building	80%	20%	none	none
10. Inspiring/Motivating	60%	40%	none	none
11. Team Building	40%	60%	none	none
12. Consensus Building	40%	60%	none	none
13. Recruiting	none	100%	none	none
14. Hiring/Firing	20%	80%	none	none
15. Conducting Meeting	40%	60%	none	none
16. Rewarding	20%	80%	none	none
17. Questioning	20%	80%	none	none
18. Disagreeing	40%	60%	none	none
19. Confronting	60	40%	none	none
20. Counseling	40%	60%	none	none
21. Mentoring	60%	40%	none	none
22. Community Building	20%	80%	none	none
23. Challenging	40%	60%	none	none
24. Trusting	60%	40%	none	none
25. Empowering	60%	40%	none	none
26. Evaluating	40%	60%	none	none
27. Managing	20%	80%	none	none
28. Leading	100%	none	none	none
29. Delegating	40%	60%	none	none
30. Discipling	60%	40%	none	none
31. Evangelizing	80%	20%	none	none
32. Correcting	40%	60%	none	none

Task Skills Inventory

Skill	necessity	needed	not needed	neutral
1. Preaching	40%	40%	none	20%
2. Teaching	100%	none	none	none
3. Researching	60%	40%	none	none
4. Communicating	100%	none	none	none
5. Mission Development	20%	80%	none	none
6. Mission Casting	none	100%	none	none
7. Vision Development	80%	20%	none	none
8. Vision Casting	80%	20%	none	none
9. Trust Building	40%	40%	none	20%
10. Strategizing	60%	40%	none	none
11. Reflecting	80%	20%	none	none
12. Time Management	20%	80%	none	none
13. Use of Technology	none	100%	none	none
14. Prioritizing	40%	60%	none	none
15. Writing	none	100%	none	none
16. General Planning	40%	60%	none	none
17. Making Presentations	40%	60%	none	none
18. Praying	100%	none	none	none
19. Budgeting	60%	40%	none	none
20. Counseling	none	100%	none	none
21. Mentoring	60%	40%	none	none

planation. The question was restated, "Can a congregation be pleasing to God without having qualified elders? The answer to that was "when the church started they qualified men and set them in. They didn't start with elders."[59] The only way to have scriptural elders is for these elders to possess the attributes listed in the Bible. Then the question was asked, "Is there anything being done here to build an eldership here, at your congregation?" One of the participants said, "We're growing into it." Then the question was asked, "How are you growing into it? What is being done to grow into it?" The answer was given that, "Qualified people are working to become elders. You got two of them sitting there, their children have to be of an age to be faithful and understand the scriptures. You can't just install a young person."[60] I then asked about exploring this a little deeper. When they say grow into the eldership, Christians have to realize that there is still something that must be done to grow. When we compare that idea to the human body we are sitting here either growing or dying. To grow into the eldership, they can't just sit here and grow into it. These men agreed with that analogy and stated that, since desiring the office is one of the qualifications we must get men to desire the office as they reach the age of being able to take the office. One of the men stated, "I am afraid where we are at we have over the years might have grown complacent in not having elders, and I am afraid that some of the older men have not formed the desire to be an elder."[61] It was also stated, "I do not think it is wrong to be absent of elders if they lack the desire to do the work…I mean they got to want it, and it has got to be their life, and there is nothing bad if they don't desire the job. It is not a job for everyone."[62] They also said they didn't think that you could change someone's mind into desiring the office. It was assumed that because the old elders were considered to be "top notch" it did not seem possible to fill their shoes. With that fear of not being able to reach the expectation of the old elders the men at the time

---

59   Ibid. Since they didn't answer the question I continued exploring their thought process and returned to the question later. See footnote 64.

60   Ibid.

61   Ibid.

62   Ibid.

would not even try. It was mentioned that they had heard teaching that some congregations would not let the apostle Peter himself be an elder because the bar is raised too high.

One of the younger participants testified that what caused him to grow was the fact that he had sat under an eldership that had all the answers. He could go to them with any kind of question or problem facing the church and they had the answer. Once they lost that last elder he found himself trying to find the answers. And because there was no one else to stand up he had to start finding answers and trying to grow. He recognized that he did not take advantage of the resource while it was available. This man stated, "What really promoted my growth all the way up is I sat under an eldership that had all the answers. I could go to them with any kind of thing that faced the church/came from the pulpit…what is unfortunate is that I did not take advantage (of it) like I should when they were here."[63] The question, "What are you doing?" was intended to discover and help them realize the need for such resources today. Within this congregation there is a whole group of young men who need to be trained to become elders and they need to ask themselves what they are doing to facilitate this training. The answer to this second line of questions is "Nothing we're doing nothing. We're trying to raise, you know, Christians, and that has been our focus. On what a disciple will be, instead of focusing on elderships."[64] I pointed out to them that you can do both and they are compatible and that when they leave this interview they need to ask themselves again, "What are we doing to make elders?" So, I asked, "Can you be pleasing to God without elders?"[65] Out of three participants one said he wondered, one nodded yes, and one is undecided. There is a difference in being scriptural and pleasing. Can one be spiritually pleasing and be in the process of gaining elders is the question.

Now looking at what was lost in the elderships' ability to mentor the next generation of elders, one of the men pointed out that first off, "Without elders, the young men lose the example and the mentor to look

---

63   Ibid.

64   Ibid.

65   Ibid. Finally answered the question, "Can you be pleasing to God without elders?"

to."[66] It was discussed how that because of our mobile society it is tough to have the type of relationship to have good mentors. It was also said that sometimes the person being mentored may not realize the gravity of what is being taught and does not capitalize on the opportunity. One man said, "I do not know if they did not mentor or maybe I was naïve enough I did not accept what they were offering, or mature enough to realize the gravity of what was going on back then."[67] Looking back, most were faithful enough, but it seemed that when deacons were installed the mentoring went away.

When asked how important were the attributes of 1 Timothy 3, Titus 1, and 1 Peter 5 when it comes to selecting elders, one of the men replied, "That it is the only grounds we have for qualifications so that's what we have to use."[68] The man next to him added, "We don't want to add our opinions to God's qualifications."[69] When looking at the role the minister has in leading the congregation, they responded, "They hoped that he would lead as one of the men and not become a pastor."[70] This is a word which has come out many times in the research of this topic. When looking at the present minister these men see him with the same responsibilities as the other men. But it is realized that with just a preacher is a bad situation and that it is very possible for things to go wrong very quickly. Through this research 34.4% of the participants go to the preacher with their problems even when there are elders. Here is the starting place for that mindset. Too many times as this congregation stated they just hope it stays in check.

The last question that was discussed was how business is conducted in this congregation in the matters of edification. The participants revealed that without elders they have to conduct business by men's business meetings. One of the participants stated, "Another problem I think we have without elders at our men's business meeting is 90% of the business being discussed is all about fixing the lights and mowing the yard

---

66   Ibid.

67   Ibid.

68   Ibid.

69   Ibid.

70   Ibid.

and we are not talking about who is taking care of the widows and doing visitation."[71] So how do they take care of edification of the congregation (teaching that would grow elders) and building up the church? They said that there they are not dealing with that. They are more business oriented. Because they use men's business meetings, they deal more with things like a deacon would do. If they had elders then the elders would deal more with the spiritual things, and what should be done for the congregation. Very little of their business meetings are dealing with edification of the congregations. When dealing with benevolence it is a little different in that when someone needs help they pretty much get help. If it is over a certain amount (unspecified) then everyone gets together and decides. If it is a lesser amount the individual just takes care of it. If it happens during the week then, because they are small, they just call a meeting for all to get together. With administration situations they just don't deal with it. They said since they don't have administrators, "We just don't do it."[72] When they were asked, "You don't have admiration issues?" they asked for a definition. I defined it as the taking care of the building, paying bills, preacher and parsonage. Then they said, "Oh, the men take care of the building, and the preacher is done by contract. The cleaning is done by a set amount of funds set aside to cover the cost of the cleaning. Whoever wants the money that week just cleans, and we give it to them."[73] If no one cleans they have an outside source which they call and they come and clean. This congregation is struggling and there are some things being done with the preacher leading the way to try and help them establish elders, but it will be a while unless they have some move in's.

The *Relational Skills* and *Task Skills* inventories found on the next two pages were handed out to those in the case study without elders, so a comparison can be made with the case study found above that had elders. I wanted to see what type of patterns could be found between men who were doing the job of elders and those who are not.

---

71   Ibid.

72   Ibid.

73   Ibid.

Relational Skills Inventory

Skill	necessity	needed	not needed	neutral
1. Listening	3/3			
2. Networking	1/3	1/3		1/3
3. Conflict Resolution	1/3			
4. Decision Making	2/3	1/3		
5. Risk Taking	1/3	1/3		1/3
6. Problem Solving	2/3	1/3		
7. Confronting	2/3	1/3		
8. Encouraging	2/3	1/3		
9. Trust Building	2/3	1/3		
10. Inspiring/Motivating	2/3	1/3		
11. Team Building	2/3	1/3		
12. Consensus Building	2/3			1/3
13. Recruiting		3/3		
14. Hiring/Firing	2/3			1/3
15. Conducting Meeting	1/3	1/3		1/3
16. Rewarding		2/3		1/3
17. Questioning		3/3		
18. Disagreeing		3/3		
19. Confronting	1/3	2/3		
20. Counseling	1/3	2/3		
21. Mentoring	1/3	2/3		
22. Community Building	2/3			1/3
23. Challenging	2/3	1/3		
24. Trusting	2/3	1/3		
25. Empowering		3/3		
26. Evaluating	2/3	1/3		
27. Managing	2/3	1/3		
28. Leading	2/3	1/3		
29. Delegating	2/3	1/3		
30. Discipling	1/3	2/3		
31. Evangelizing	2/3	1/3		
32. Correcting	2/3	1/3		

Task Skills Inventory

Skill	necessity	needed	not needed	neutral
1. Preaching	1/3	1/3	1/3	
2. Teaching	2/3	1/3		
3. Researching	1/3	1/3		1/3
4. Communication	2/3	1/3		
5. Mission Development	2/3			1/3
6. Mission Casting	2/3			1/3
7. Vision Development	2/3			1/3
8. Vision Casting	2/3			1/3
9. Trust Building	2/3	1/3		
10. Strategizing	2/3	1/3		
11. Reflecting	1/3	2/3		
12. Time Management		3/3		
13. Use of Technology			2/3	1/3
14. Prioritizing	1/3	2/3		
15. Writing		1/3		2/3
16. General Planning		3/3		
17. Making Presentations		1/3		2/3
18. Praying	2/3	1/3		
19. Budgeting	1/3	1/3		1/3
20. Counseling	2/3	1/3		
21. Mentoring	2/3	1/3		

Summary

In this chapter, I have recorded the data that has been obtained through the individual participants' survey and interviews as well as the case studies of congregations with and without elders. As a part of the case studies, there is also included data which resulted from *Task Skills Inventory*, as well as *Relational Skills Inventory*, given to each participant of the case studies. This survey shows the difference in the mindset of those who do not have elders and elders who strive to replicate self by training and mentoring from within the congregation they serve. In chapter 5 the analysis of this data will be presented looking for reoccurring topics and ideas as to why there is a decline in the leadership within the church of Christ.

Chapter 5:

Analysis of Data

In this chapter I will give my analysis of the data as collected through the surveys, interviews, and case studies which were presented in Chapter 4. In finding the common themes and ideas of those who participated in the research I will show some reasons found leading to the current decline in church leadership. A perspective held by the highest percentage of participants that explains the decline seems to concern how the elders are viewed by the church. It is a fact that there is a belief that a congregation does not have to have elders to be pleasing. This belief has brought a digression of the spiritual maturity of the church, the lack of mentoring by the previous and existing elders, and a lack of communication among the brethren. The data that was compiled showed five major patterns which were assessed. These are: how the elders are viewed, the attitude that a congregation need not have elders to be pleasing to God, the spiritual maturity of the church is weakening, the lack of mentoring of the next generation of elders, and a lack of communication between the elder and his flock.

How Churches View Their Elders

Data from the survey by individuals showed that 55.1% viewed the elders as administrators. Only 44.8% saw the elders as shepherds. They saw the elder as not leading the sheep but rather micromanaging the congregation and truly dealing with the administrative duties instead of leading the flock. Yet, nearly all agree that the biblical image of the elder is the shepherd. When the amount of love, respect, and admiration that the elder receives is discussed, the data showed that this was based upon the work the elder did or didn't do. Because of this, 51.7 % showed that they do not receive the respect that elders did in the 20th Century because they are not shepherding the flock but rather acting as administrators. 27.5% would say yes, the elder today is respected as much as those in the last century, leaving 20% that would take the neutral stance. This means when the elder does the work of shepherding the flock he is loved and cherished for his service. It also addresses the question of, "Why has the eldership today lost the ability to lead the congregation in their spiritual formation?" The lack of respect has brought about a lack of leadership. Along this same line is the fact that the culture of today does not respect any authority. This has flowed over into the church. Since we are not teaching our young people to respect authority, the elders of the church lose respect just by being a leader. This has hindered many men from seeking the work of an elder.

Another part of the equation is how the younger men think of themselves as being better educated than the older generation. Therefore, when elders try to teach or correct, the young adults feel that they are better schooled to understand the Bible and shun the advice of the elder. As congregations lose the respect and admiration for the elder, this has a direct correlation with men desiring to put themselves and their families in the position to be verbally, mentally and physically abused for the sake of the congregation. Because of this, the first attribute of the elder is already eliminated from most qualified men, the desire to be an elder. Many today have forgotten Hebrews 13:17, "Obey them that have the rule over you, and submit yourselves: for they watch for your souls, as they that must give account, that they may do it with joy, and not with grief: for that is unprofitable for you."

While secular education of the younger generation may be more advanced it does little to teach the Bible, or the knowledge gleaned from years of study and a lifetime of experience. These younger members also have lost sight of the fact of that the Christian is to, "Let the elders that rule well be counted worthy of double honour, especially they who labour in the word and doctrine" (1 Tm 5:17). This is also one of the reasons that elders today need to mentor the next generation so that they will know how to handle not only the good times as a shepherd, but the bad times as well.

The attitude that a congregation does not have to have elders to be pleasing to God

It is so important to understand that the local congregation must be pleasing to God in order to be acceptable to Him. It cannot just be pleasing to itself and be acceptable to God. In this point, there is a mixed signal being given how to be pleasing to Him. 28 out of the 29 interviewed state that it was extremely important for the church to have elders. Yet, eleven out of twenty-nine worships without elders. Nearly 38% do not have elders and when asked if they can be pleasing to God without elders, 9% of those surveyed claim that a congregation can be pleasing to God without an eldership.

In the case study without elders the same question was asked. They all answered, "Yes," they believed it could because if there are no qualified men you can't install elders. In turn the question was asked in a private setting if a person could be pleasing without being baptized. They all stated absolutely not! I said well, the same Bible that says, "He that believeth and is baptized shall be saved; but he that believeth not shall be damned" (Mk 16:16) also says, "For this cause left I thee in Crete, that thou shouldest set in order the things that are wanting, and ordain elders in every city, as I had appointed thee" (Ti 1:5). I agree fully that we dare not appoint men who are unqualified. But I see many congregations who take the mindset that since we don't have qualified men we will just work off men's business meetings and then never work to develop and grow qualified men. That might mean we have to go out and convert and teach men how to be elders, but we cannot just go fifteen years (as in the case of the case study group) without developing elders.

Can a congregation be pleasing to God without elders? Yes, for a short time while they establish elders, but not indefinitely. And many of the congregation today have grown accustomed to not having elders.

When eleven out of twenty-nine do not have elders, and have not for over ten years there is a pattern showing. They do not discuss how to have elders and that is why without selecting the congregation for this study there are four out of the nine without elders. Out of nine congregations surveyed only two have programs in place trying to train up the next generation of elders. There is a correlation between the attitude of being able to please God without an eldership and the question of why the number of congregations without elderships has multiplied. If one can be pleasing without elders, then why go through the trouble to train men to take on the responsibility. This is a mindset I totally disagree with. The Lord's church must establish elderships as the above Bible verse shows.

Along with this point, almost 38% of the data collected showed that when congregations don't have elders it brings about chaos and apathy in the congregation. The chance of error and false teaching increases. And if they do not turn into a denominational frame of mind, they slowly but surely shrivel up and die from a lack of good, solid feeding. Remembering that 38% have not had elders for > 10 years, it is not surprising that 72% of those interviewed stated the church is not as knowledgeable as in the past century. This alone should stop most congregations from going one day more than necessary without an eldership. It also can slow down the decision-making process as already discussed in the previous chapter. The decision to appoint elders is one of those decisions. In the case study of the congregation without elders, it was reported that over the years they had become complacent in not having elders and that is one of the reasons they had not been developing them until recently.

So, one of the main reasons there is a decline is because even though most say having elders is extremely important (96%) when it comes to actions many are comfortable without them. The reason it is comfortable not having elders is the fact that without them there is no accountability. The individuals can do what they want when they want without any repercussions from the church. Of those interviewed, 41.3% believed elders dealt with problems at the building and not with the individual's life. That leaves 58.6% of participants that see elders as having an input on the individual's life. Unfortunately, even when there are not elders God still holds the individual accountable. Paul reminded the Romans of this same fact, "So then every one of us shall give account of himself to God" (Rom 14:12). God gives the church watchmen (Ez 3:17) to warn the church when danger arrives. That is the danger of false teaching, or when sin enters into the church, the shepherd is to warn the flock. Without elders the members are able to do what feels good to them instead of what God has demanded. Throughout the Bible God instructs his children to heed the wisdom of the "hoary head." Moses, speaking for God, reminds Israel that "Thou shalt rise up before the hoary head, and honour the face of the old man, and fear thy God: I am the LORD" (Lv 19:32). This is the reason God used the elders of Israel from the Old Testament as the example for those who would have the oversight of the church. A man who has raised his kids to be believing children, and has ruled well his own house that he might know how to rule in God's house (1 Tm 3:4-6). When people are left to their own devices sin is never far away. In just a 40 day period of time, while Moses was on the mountain, the people of Israel defiled themselves. Too many today enjoy being without elders so they may have religion their way.

Spiritual Maturity of the Church is Weakening

In the first century it was the elders who were appointed to feed the flock, not preachers. The spiritual maturity of a congregation lay directly upon the shoulders of the elders. Paul instructed the Ephesian elders, "Take heed therefore unto yourselves, and to all the flock, over the which the Holy Ghost hath made you overseers, to feed the church of God, which he hath purchased with his own blood" (Acts 20:28). With many of the congregations today not having elderships there is a lack of spiritual formation. As shown in the data, 93.1% of those interviewed saw a direct correlation between the elders and their ability to teach and feed the flock to the spiritual maturity of the congregation. So, in congregations where there is not an eldership the congregation is not growing spiritually. How then can they develop elders? Also with that in mind only 31.6%, said that the elders today where able to teach and train as well as the elders of the 20th Century. About 59% of those interviewed see the elders as inadequate in their teaching abilities. This would also correlate with the 72.1% who see the spiritual maturity of the church today as strong as those in the last century. This lack of Bible knowledge not only makes today's church vulnerable to error and false hood; but, it also shows why there is a short fall in having qualified men to enter into the work of the shepherd. And, with the weakening of the shepherd's ability to teach, they also lose the ability to mentor the next generation of elder. Along this line they also lose the ability to strengthen the church which starts the cycle all over again.

The research noted that 100% of the participants saw the attributes for the eldership as being vital. 100%! But then almost 1/3 said that it depends on how you interpret those attributes and that we cannot find elders because we are looking for the perfect man. I see this as another place where the spiritual weakness of many of the congregations keeps them from developing elders according to the Bible. Literally 50% of the participants don't think the elders of today have the biblical knowledge of those in the last century. Maybe that is why they cannot see how to apply the attributes of the elders to a practical application of establishing elders. I see this as one of the reasons that an elder has to be apt to teach. When elders will stand up and teach young men the attributes of 1 Timothy 3:1-7 and Titus 1:6-9 they will see those "perfect" men. We will see men who have a desire to serve God and shepherd the flock as God would have it. The attributes as mentioned multiple times in the interviews (Appendix A) will become a part of the lives of the young men who will be taking up the mantle as they become of age to be shepherds. As it is, today many argue over the attributes because those whom they would like to see in the eldership role are not and cannot qualify for the office. In many congregations the office of the elder has become a popularity contest and the one placed in the office is not based on qualification, but what the individual can do for me. With unqualified men being placed into the office of elder, we see the weakening of teaching, the lack of standing for truth, and the congregation becomes less mature in their spiritual formation. With this weakening there is a natural decline of the eldership.

Mentoring the next generation

Every secular book on management and leadership places a very high premium on mentoring as a way of maintaining a healthy leadership for business. The same is true in the church. In the case study with the congregation with ten elders they give a lot of credit for having an eldership for more than 100 years to the personal mentoring of the young men to replicate the existing elders. In the interviews, 96.5% stated that it was vital to keeping strong eldership. The case study without elders confirmed that one of the things which did not take place fifteen years ago was mentoring, along with general teachings on elders. Yet, I found in the data that today 37.9% do not see a desire to mentor from the present elders. Some 36% of the participants said they do not see the present elders training or mentoring the young men in their congregation. Another 30% say that the elders they know not only do not have the desire to mentor but also do not possess the ability to mentor. This is also shown in how the elders today in many instances are viewed in not doing their job, as well as the spiritual weakness of these elders and not being able to teach. While I see this as a vitally important part of being an elder, I think most of the time it is missed because of neglect or oversight instead of inability. But, without today's elders mentoring to the next generation I am afraid we will continue to see a decline in elders simply because they will not know how to lead as God would have them to. It was for this reason that Paul would instruct Timothy, "And the things that thou hast heard of me among many witnesses, the same commit thou to faithful men, who shall be able to teach others also. Thou therefore endure hardness, as a good soldier of Jesus Christ." (2 Tm 2:2-3) The true biblical example of the mentoring process.

Sometimes, when elders are appointed there are older elders in place which can help teach by on the job training how to shepherd the flock. Mentoring helps the younger men understand and have an expectation of what the job will entail. Mentoring from an early age also helps to ensure that the young men grow in the nurture and admonition of the Lord. Many of our young men disqualify themselves long before they ever are considered for the office simply because they are left to themselves and to the ways of the world which they have been taught in school and by television. Elders today are in a battle to replicate self. If they don't start the day they take office, they will one day wake up to see that there is no one following in their tracks. George Jones sang the song *"Who's Gonna to Fill Their Shoes?"* Elders today must ask that same question.

Communication of the eldership

One of the most damaging problems–behind the lack of biblical knowledge–is a failure to communicate. All too often a congregation has no idea of what the vision of their local congregation is. They have no idea of what the mission of the church is. What do the elders see happening to and for the church in which they serve? This is one of the reasons given for turning into a pastoral church. This pastoral church is not the biblical model found in the Scriptures, but rather the denominational practice of the preacher having the leadership role in place of the elders. The biblical model is when pastors (elders) are the ones who lead the congregation. When asked about who dealt with problems, 51.6% said either the preacher or the men and 34.8% said preacher. That leaves 48.2% saying elders tend to the problems in the church. When those interviewed were asked why, it was often stated that the preacher is easy to find. When asked who addresses spiritual matters of the congregation, 82.7% said the preacher. The same reason was given: because they knew where he was.

A simple question was asked in the interviews: *"When do your elders meet?"* About 63% did not know when their elders meet. In fact, in the interviews who knew, were seven men who were elders, deacons, or preachers. Even the elders and deacons' wives did not know.

The case study with elders stood out in their discussion on communication compared to the other participants, first and foremost was how could they better communicate with the flock. They exhibited a lot of energy in communicating through bulletins, announcements, Facebook, website, and PowerPoint announcements before worship. They also made a point that each worship service was begun by an elder, and each worship service was closed by an elder. When I asked why they did that, they answered so that the congregation would see them as much or more than the preacher. The elders wanted the members to know them and feel free to go to elders. As a side note I went to a Wednesday worship there and just casually asked members if they knew when their elders meet. One hundred percent said, "Every Tuesday night and on Sunday afternoon at 3:30pm-5 pm three of the 10 are at the building to meet or help anyone who needs them. This is a congregation of over 600, and has had an active eldership for over 100 years. I think the record speaks clear. If you are communicating with your flock and they know your voice you will continually grow stronger and closer.

The data from the interviews show that four of the five elderships represented do not communicate with their flock, so they slowly but surely decline in spirit and numbers. Jesus the chief shepherd taught this lesson in a very clear manner. He said, "But he that entereth in by the door is the shepherd of the sheep. To him the porter openeth; and the sheep hear his voice: and he calleth his own sheep by name, and leadeth them out." (Jn 10:2-3) The sheep will not follow a stranger and if the shepherds do not talk to their flocks then the sheep do not know their voice and will go their own way.

One of the ways the aforementioned elders communicated with their flock was that every service was began by one of the elders and then that elder led them in prayer. In addition, every service is closed by an elder who then leads them in prayer. They reported that this is one of the ways that they made sure that they were known by their flock. The communication exchange between the elder and his congregation shows the congregation that the elder has a clear understanding about what he intends to communicate. This compares well to a teaching role. If when the teacher is through the class can recite back verbatim, then all they have done is memorized and true understanding does not have to be a part of the exchange. But, if the student can explain in their own words the lesson to be learned, then you know that they have understood and can replicate the teacher. When elders communicate to their congregations, there is less likely to be misunderstanding and the eldership knows they are sending clear signals. This is done by remembering whom the elders are speaking to and their age groups, and asking for feedback to give the congregation a sense of ownership to that which is being communicated. Without communication then, even if it is not intended, often the congregation will see the elders as lording over the flock. It is thought that perhaps because of the lack of communication between the elder and the congregation and the preacher having a more personal relationship with the individuals in the congregation that they turn to the preacher instead. So, the data is showing a weaker church, in most cases today because of the lack of teaching, communications and relationships established between the elders and the congregation. As a result of this weakening many congregations seem to be dying on the vine.

Recommendations

What can we change that will help curb the decline in eldership? To curb the decline as seen in this study, it is suggested that better methods of training and mentoring future elders be developed. As these are being developed, a return to stronger teaching and preaching in our churches needs to take place to help revive the spiritual health of the congregations. We must learn to strengthen our personal relationships with not only each other but also with our shepherds. And there is a vital need for us and the shepherds alike to learn to communicate one with the other. This would not only help in working with our elders but also in avoiding the many problems and pitfalls which plague our congregations, which stem from our lack of communicating with each other. It is only when we strive to have scriptural elders in every church the world over that God will bless the church in its endeavors.

With the mentoring of our young men to become elders, there will be an increase in Bible study. This in turn will help grow the next generation of elders in the knowledge of the scriptures. Along with this training the next generation of elder should learn to be not only more active, but more adapt to the art of teaching. According to the research, as they become more adapt to teaching and leading the flock in its spiritual maturity they will gain the respect and love of that flock as in times past. Also, as the elders grow in their skills of leadership they will also discover how to train and mentor that next generation. It is also necessary that the current eldership learn that it is not a bad thing to replicate self. From the first day they take on the work of an elder, they should be looking and training their replacement.

To break the current trend of decline in the oversight of elders we must instill in our young men the desire to become leaders in the Lord's church. I see one of the problems here is in our raising of our children. Parents tend to want their kids to go to secular schools to become doctors, lawyers, accountants, and computer programmers. It is recommended that parents join with the current leadership in showing the rewards of becoming not only elders, but also preachers, both of which are in decline.

It is also recommended that elders spend time learning how to plan, set goals, and then communicate those goals to the congregation. As was shown in the review of literature, it is a necessity for congregations to take ownership of the goals of that congregation if they are to be successful in accomplishing those goals. The research showed that there is a severe problem in the eldership's ability to communicate well with the congregation. No organization can survive the lack of communication. Just as a marriage will fail if the spouses do not communicate, so too have many congregations today fallen due to the lack of communication.

I would also recommend that we leave the denominational platform of the pastoral church where the preacher is doing the work of the elders. The preacher teaches all the classes, he is the one who visits the sick, he councils with those having problems, and in general hears most of the complaints. These areas of works are the elder's responsibility. The preacher is the preachers. He is to herald the Gospel, ministering to the community. The elders need to return to the biblical form of shepherding, overseeing the needs of the congregations, and demand that preachers go back to the job of preaching. In the research it was shown that the main reason that elders today do not have the respect and love shown to the elders of the past is this lack of doing the work of the shepherd. This in turn has the effect of causing the young men not to desire the office of the elder seeing the lack of love for the present men. That means this aspect may be the one most important thing we can do to slow the decline of the eldership.

I can see many side studies that should be done in the future such as doing demographic studies to see what the millennial mindset contributes to this decline. That is 36 years of losing sight of biblical morality, work ethics, and commitment all of which have surfaced in this study but could not be fully developed. The generation gaps in technology, education, mobility, and communication all needs to be looked at. Also, another good study might look at how much does secular education play in this decline. I am sure the humanist aspect of core curriculum has affected this decline of leadership as has situation ethics.

Along this same line of study, we need to look at the influence that the modern family plays in the decline of the eldership. With the societal views of discipline and the lack of biblical teaching on how to train up the child, many see a casual approach to religion as the way to go. Our young adults have forgotten that actions have consequences. They have been raised receiving participation awards for just showing up and there is a segment of the church that equates that with proper service to God. This was expressed by the large congregation's elders as they discussed the lack of commitment with the younger men. These younger men will work, but only in areas that suit them. It was mentioned in the research that when the men are pressed they just change membership.

That leads to the mobility of the membership. It is recommended that we look at how mobile church is today. If the members do not like the teaching or the elders require faithfulness, those involved just move. In years gone by when members moved letters were sent out to address the faithfulness (or not) of the member. This was done to let the new eldership know what they were getting. Congregations need to start communicating with each other as members move around in this mobile society. When problem members can just move on then their soul is still in danger and their problems are now the concern of two congregations. First the concern of the eldership with whom the problem began and then the new congregation where the problem was taken. I believe that this added burden on the elders is a possible contributing factor to the decrease of elderships as well as the weakening of the spiritual formation of the congregation.

To curb the decline as seen in this study, it is suggested that better methods of training and mentoring future elders be developed. As these are being developed, a return to stronger teaching and preaching in our churches needs to take place to help revive the spiritual health of the congregations. We must learn to strengthen our personal relationships with not only each other but also with our shepherds. And there is a vital need for us and the shepherds alike to learn to communicate one with the other. This would not only help in working with our elders but also in avoiding the many problems and pitfalls which plague our congregations, which stem from our lack of communicating with each other. It is only when we strive to have scriptural elders in every church the world over that God will bless the church in its endeavors.

Conclusion

The grounded theory which the research has established, points to some of the reasons for the decline in church leadership and consists of at least five problems. First, the way in which elders are viewed within the congregation today as administrators instead of shepherds. Second, the attitude that the church can be pleasing to God while not establishing elderships. Third, a weakening of spiritual maturity in the church because of a lack of teaching and preaching which results in unqualified men for the office. Fourth, a lack of desire and ability by the current elderships to mentor the next generation of elders. And finally, and perhaps the strongest, is a lack of communication between the elders and their flock. This, I am sure is not even close to all the reasons for the decline, but these are the ones that seem to be the main causes shown by the research.

When I started to look at some of the factors which contributed to the decline in the eldership in the twenty-first century there were four questions which were the driving force of the study. Each of these four questions was addressed from different angles of the surveys, interviews, and case studies. Once the data was collected, I looked to find common themes, patterns of thoughts, and words, and then, observed how they pertained to the questions.

The first question I wanted to examine was, "Why has the number of congregations without elderships multiplied?" The interviews substantiated that 37.9% of those participating do not have elders. During the interview, many of the participants said they had noticed that in traveling, more and more congregations do not have elders. In the surveys collected, 89% said that congregations with qualified men must have elders to be pleasing to God. In the interviews, 96% said it was important for the local congregation to have elders. Yet almost half of the congregations do not have elders and that number is growing. Most of the congregations without elders work off the men's business meeting system with the preacher being the main person who handles all problems and situations. It was noted in the interviews that the pastoral system is a growing phenomenon as members bring their denominational backgrounds into the church. This mindset is one of the leading contributing factors to the decline. The case studies confirmed this. The case study with the eldership reported that they had done an in-house study which showed that starting at age fifty-five and going down that many men had lost the will to be committed to the work of an elder. They said the men of the congregation were willing to work and help in nearly any aspect, but when it comes to desiring the office of an elder they would not commit themselves to be responsible. Along with the lack of commitment, this younger age group has lost their respect for not just elders but for anything: authority, our country, the flag, everything except themselves. They want to be respected and have things their way but will not apply that respect to others and that causes the desire to be an elder to be lost.

The second question is, "What has the eldership today lost in the ability to mentor the next generation of elders?" This question is very closely related to the third question, "Why has the eldership today lost the desire to mentor the next generation of elders?" So, we will look at them together. In the section of review of literature, it was pointed out that one of the reasons that many elders today are not mentoring is because they have a fear of transparency. When an individual mentors another he has to show his true self to the one being taught. The data showed this to be true. Because many of the elders today are weak or unqualified they are unwilling to, not only mentor the next generation of elders, but are uncomfortable even teaching the laity. Of those interviewed 58.6% reported the belief that elders today are unable to teach or defend the Word of God as those in the past were. This has the effect of not only weakening the next eldership but also the spiritual formation of the church. In the case that a weakened congregation loses its eldership, then there is no one who can mentor the next generation. Many also do not understand what it means to mentor. In the case study of the congregation without elders the idea of mentoring was installing elders. As the number of elders decrease, so does the number of qualified mentors. This means when a group of men are finally installed as elders they have to learn how to lead by the school of hard knocks. It was also reported that with the mentoring process the desire to serve is instilled into the men who are being trained. This alone is one of the main detriments to the elderships of the future, the lack of desire. In the surveys, 63% said that the desire to become elders of the Lord's church has been lost. Men simply do not desire the office. The review of literature also discusses how that some men refuse to mentor for fear of being replaced. This thought process came up time and again in the interview process. In this study out of nine congregations, only two were found to have any type of formal mentoring classes or programs in place. One of the things that should be considered after the completion of this study is how the church can implement mentoring programs to help develop and train young men, before they have disqualified themselves to have the desire and be the elder of the future. While 93% agree that all congregations need to develop elders, only 37.9% see any kind of mentoring or teaching on the eldership being done.

The fourth question I wanted to look at was, "Why has the eldership today lost the ability to lead congregations in their spiritual formations and what affects has it had on the local congregation?" In 1 Peter 5:2,3 we read, "Feed the flock of God which is among you, taking the oversight thereof, not by constraint, but willingly; not for filthy lucre, but of a ready mind; neither as being lords over God's heritage, but being ensamples to the flock." The elder's work is to feed and oversee the flock; many of the congregations I interviewed, elders are not allowed to oversee and are not capable of feeding. This is born out in the data I have collected. While 84% of those surveyed said they are encouraged to study, 72% see the church weaker today than it was in the twentieth century. The laity is not studying God's Word and the elders are not teaching it. This is another reason we have become a pastoral church, where the preacher is the feeder and defender of the body. This should not be the case. As the verse given above shows the elders should be overseeing the flock and feeding by actively teaching the congregation the ways of the Lord. The reason given in the data that elders today do not receive the respect and love of those in times past is because they are not doing the job that God has given them. Instead of shepherds they are administrators. This has driven a wedge between elderships and the congregation they are intended to lead. Also, coming out of the interview and collaborating with the review of literature is the lack of communication between the elders and their flock. I asked the simple question, "When do your elders meet?" and out of the 19 which worshiped under an eldership only seven knew. All the ones who knew were elders, deacons, or preachers. Even the elders' wives got it wrong. To lead one must be able to effectively communicate the goals and directions of the congregation as planned by the shepherds. Then they must find a way to allow the congregation to claim those goals for themselves and then lead them in the fulfilling of those goals. This is a theme that not only ran through the data collected but also ran through the review of literature. Jesus said, "And when he putteth forth his own sheep, he goeth before them, and the sheep follow him: for they know his voice." (Mt 10:4) The reason the elders today have lost the ability to lead their congregations in spiritual formation is because the congregation does not know their voice. In the case study with the large congregation with elders they credited their successes in the spiritual formation of the congregation there to the fact that all ten of the shepherds there are active in teaching classes and being known by the flock. An elder opens each worship service with a prayer and ends each with a prayer. In the interview one of the elders stated they know my voice and they follow. That is in accord with John 10:4 in which Jesus also said, "He goeth before them." Some elders today are not going before them. They have left the job of feeding the flock to the preacher, many of which are young and have little to no life experiences to draw from. When error is brought into a congregation seldom do you see elders standing up and contending for the faith. Often it is left up to the preacher who may or may not recognize the ending result to just a little bit of falsehood. Elders a century ago stood firm for the truth. As I witnessed in debates and services preachers teaching error were sat down by elders who would correct the error and then lead his sheep to safety. Today because the congregations see the preacher as being educated in Scriptures, he is the one the congregation follows. Many times, in the interview the reason given for the elders losing their ability to lead was that his biblical knowledge was not on par with the preacher. Therefore, the preacher was looked to for answers of both the biblical and physical problems.

Looking at the data, the elders today are losing the ability to lead their congregation in both its spiritual formation as well as in their personal lives. In many ways this is due to their own fault. More research needs to be done on how we can educate our young to the point where they are once again known as "walking Bibles." This is one of my goals for this research to move forward and develop some type of training manual to help congregations to train up future generations. Also, I want to help parents learn the importance of instilling the desire into our young men to be elders and our young ladies to be elder's wives. I would also like to find a way to help the current elders to mentor and replicate self. In many cases this will have to begin by removing the fear of being replaced and learning how to be transparent in their life and work. And finally, I would like to help preachers learn how to say that is not my job. You need to go talk to the elders, taking the pastoral church and transforming it back into the true biblical church where the elder leads the congregation, feeding the flock, while the preacher ministers and evangelizes the community by preaching the Gospel of Jesus Christ.

Last words

At the end of this study I would love to further explore the relationship of the millennial mindset and the effect it has on the eldership. A generation gap has been discussed for decades, but looking at some of the work that George Barna and others have done, the gap seems to be getting wider instead of being narrowed. In the church of Christ, we must find a way to close the gap and bring our spiritual family back together. We need to learn how to communicate with each other and learn how to have the true agape love one for another, instead of having all of these man-made divisions. Paul told Titus to, "Set in order the things that are wanting, and ordain elders in every city, as I had appointed thee." (Ti 1:5) It is time that we find a way to bring men back to the Bible and teach them how to be Scriptural elders so that our congregation might once again be "in order." That will only be done by prayer and by returning to the old paths as instructed in Jeremiah 6:16 "where is the good way."

Bibliography

Agee, Bob R. "Servant Leadership as an Effective Approach to Leadership in the Church." *Southwestern Journal of Theology* 43, no 3 (2001): 7-18.

Anderson, Lynn. *They Smell Like Sheep. Vol. I Spiritual Leadership for the 21st Century.* New York: Howard Books, 1997.

Auerbach Carl F. and Louise B. Silverstein. *Qualitative Data: An Introduction to Coding and Analysis.* New York: New York University Press, 2003.

Barensten, Jack. "Church Leadership as Adaptive Identity Construction in a Changing Social Context." *Journal of Religious Leadership* 14, no. 2 (September 2015): 49-79.

Bass, Bernard M. and Ruth Bass. *The Bass Handbook of Leadership, Theory, Research, & Managerial Applications, Fourth Edition.* New York: Free Press, 2008.

Boa, Kenneth. *The Perfect Leaders Practicing the Leadership Traits of God.* Eugene: WIPF & Stock Publishing, 2006.

Burch, Michael J., Patricia Wails, and Randy Mills. "Perceptions of Administrators' Servant Leadership Qualities at A Christian University: A Descriptive Study." *Education* 1315, no. 4 (2015): 399-404.

Callahan, Sharon Henderson. "Shifting Images of Church Invite New Leadership Frames." *Journal of Religious Leadership* 1, no. 1 (2002): 55-82.

Croft, Brian. *The Pastor's Ministry: Biblical Priorities for Faithful Shepherds*. Grand Rapids: Zondervan, 2015.

Dever, Mark E. "Ecclesiological Issues for the Local Church Today." *Bibliotheca Sacra* 172 (October-December 2015): 387-397.

Dollhoph, Erica J., and Christopher Scheitle. "Decline and Conflict: Causes of Consequences of Leadership Transitions in Religious Congregations." *Journal for The Scientific Study of Religion* 52, no. 4 (2013): 675-697.

Earley, Dave, and Ben Gutierrez. *Ministry is...: How to Serve Jesus with Passion and Confidence*. Nashville: B&H Publishing Group, 2010.

Fairholm, Gilbert W. *Capturing the Heart of Leadership*. Westport, CT: Praeger, 1997.

Ferguson, Everett. "Authority and Tenure of Elders." *Restoration Quarterly* 18, no. 3 (1975): 142-150.

Ferguson, Everett. *The Church of Christ: A Biblical Ecclesiology for Today*. Grand Rapids: Eerdmans, 1997.

Fisher, David. *The 21st Century Pastor*. Grand Rapids: Zondervan, 1996.

Greenleaf, Robert K. *Servant Leadership: A Journey into The Nature of Legitimate Power & Greatness*. New York: Paulist Press, 1977.

Harris-Harrison, Delores E. "Leadership Challenges of Churches in Transition: A Study of Three Churches." *Journal of Unification Studies* 13 (2012): 175-190.

Hayward, R. David, and Neal Krause. "Voluntary Leadership Roles in Religious Groups and Rates of Change in Functional Status During Older Adulthood." *Journal of Behavioral Medicine* 37, no. 2 (June 2014): 543-552.

Hirsch, Alan. *The Forgotten Ways: Reactivating the Missional Church.* Grand Rapids: Brazos Press, 2006.

Holderread, Kenneth O. "The Role of Eldering and The Christian Community," *Brethren Life and Thought* 24, no. 4 (1979): 205-209.

Leedy, Paul D., and Jeanne Ellis Ormrod. *Practical Research Planning and Design*, 11th ed. Old Tappan: Pearson, 2014.

Lussier, Robert N., and Christopher F. Achua. *Leadership: Theory, Application, & Skill Development.* Mason, OH: South-Western, 2013

Malphurs, Aubrey. *Advanced Strategic Planning.* Grand Rapids: Baker, 2005.

Malphurs, Aubrey, and Will Mancini. *Building Leaders; Blueprints for Developing Leadership at every Level of Your Church.* Grand Rapids: Baker Books, 2004.

Malphurs, Aubrey. *Maximizing Your Effectiveness: How to Discover and Develop Your Divine Design.* Grand Rapids: Baker Books, 2006.

Maple, John T. "Discord in The Mother Church: The Failure of Leadership in the Later Years of the Church of Christ in Barker Gate, Nottingham." *Restoration Quarterly* 55, no 4 (2013): 213-224.

Mayhue, Richard L. "Authentic Spiritual Leadership." *The Master's Seminary Journal* 22/2 (Fall 2011): 213-224.

Penwell, Derek. "The Changing Role of Elders in the Disciples of Christ." *Lexington Theological Quarterly* 35, no.2 (2000): 63-82.

Robertson, Archibald Thomas. *Word Pictures in the New Testament Vol. IV The Epistles of Paul.* Nashville: Broadman, 1931.

Rochford, E. Burke Jr, and Kendra Bailey. "Almost Heaven: Leadership, Decline and the Transformation of New Vrindaban." *Nova Religio* 9, no. 3 (February 2006): 6-23.

Sensing, Tim. *Qualitative Research; A Multi-Methods Approach to Projects for Doctor or Ministry Theses.* Eugene, OR: Wipf and Stock Publishers, 2011.

Sims, Bryan D., and J. Paulo Lopes. "Spiritual Leadership and Transformational Change Across Cultures: the SLI Leadership Incubator." *Journal of Religious Leadership.* vol. 10, no. 2 (Fall, 2011): 59-86.

Soanes, Catherine, and Angus Stevenson. *Concise Oxford English Dictionary.* New York: Oxford University Press, 2008.

Stanley, Paul D., and J. Robert Clinton. *Connecting: The Mentoring Relationships You Need to Succeed in Life.* Colorado Springs: Navpress, 1992.

Stark, Rodney. "Why Religious Movements Succeed or Fail: A Revised General Model." *Journal of Contemporary Religion.* (1996) 133-146.

Strauch, Alexander. *Biblical Elders: An Urgent Call to Restore Biblical Church Leadership.* Littleton: Lewis and Roth, 1995.

Turner, J.J. *Christian Leadership Handbook: How to be Worth Following.* West Monroe: Howard Publishing Co., 1982.

Vincent, Marvin R. *Word Studies in the New Testament.* Mclean: MacDonald Publishing Company, 1888.

Wilson, John F. "Saints, Shepherds, Preachers, and Scholars: Leadership Crisis in Churches of Christ." *Restoration Quarterly* 34, no. 3 (1991): 129-134.

Yeakley, Flavil R. Jr. *Church Leadership & Organization.* Nashville: Christian Communications, 1989.

Yin, Robert K. *Case Study Research, Design and Methods.* Los Angeles: Sage Publication Ltd. 2014.

Appendix A:

Comparison of Elder Qualifications

1 Timothy 3:2-7

1. Above reproach
2. Husband of one wife
3. Temperate
4. Prudent
5. Respectable
6. Hospitable
7. Able to teach
8. Not addicted to wine
9. Not pugnacious
10. Gentle
11. Uncontentious
12. Free of the love of money
13. Manages his home
14. Not a new convert
15. Good reputation from without

Titus 1:6-9

1. Above Reproach
2. Husband of one wife
3. Believing children
4. Not self-willed
5. Not quick-tempered
6. Not addicted to wine
7. Not pugnacious
8. Not fond of sordid gain
9. Hospitable
10. Lover of what is good
11. Sensible
12. Just
13. Devout
14. Self-controlled
15. Holds fast the Word

1 Peter 5:1-3

1. Not under compulsion
2. Not for sordid gain/eager
3. Not lording over

Church Leadership Survey

When completing the following survey, please answer the questions based upon the four-point continuum from *Highly Agree* to *Highly Disagree*. These are opinion questions; there are no right or wrong answers.

1. The congregation I attend encourages me to make time each day to study the Word of God.

    Highly Agree   *Agree*   *Disagree*   *Highly Disagree*

2. I believe a congregation with qualified men does not have to have an eldership to be pleasing to God.

    Highly Agree   *Agree*   *Disagree*   *Highly Disagree*

3. I believe Paul instructed all congregations to develop elders.

    Highly Agree   *Agree*   *Disagree*   *Highly Disagree*

4. I believe the eldership has biblical authority to make decisions for the local congregation.

    Highly Agree   *Agree*   *Disagree*   *Highly Disagree*

5. I believe elders today have as much biblical knowledge as those of the Twentieth Century.

    Highly Agree   *Agree*   *Disagree*   *Highly Disagree*

6. Elders I know spend time teaching young men how to be good elders.

    Highly Agree   *Agree*   *Disagree*   *Highly Disagree*

7. Elders today are held up in high esteem.

    Highly Agree   *Agree*   *Disagree*   *Highly Disagree*

8. I believe elders today have the ability and the desire to mentor the next generation of elders.

    Highly Agree   *Agree*   *Disagree*   *Highly Disagree*

9. Men today have a desire to become elders.

    Highly Agree   *Agree*   *Disagree*   *Highly Disagree*

10. Elders today are known for leading the congregation in its spiritual growth.

    Highly Agree   *Agree*   *Disagree*   *Highly Disagree*

Appendix C:

Church Leadership Interview Questions

1. How important do you believe it is to have elders in the local congregation? How does it affect the congregation not having qualified elders?
2. Does the congregation where you attend have elders?
3. Is the spiritual formation of the church as strong today as in times past? What do you base this observation on?
4. Is there a desire to mentor the next generation of elders by the present elders?
5. Is it important for the elders to mentor the next generation of elders? How do you see this being done, or not being done?
6. In their ability to teach and train, do you see today's elders as qualified as those in the past? What do you base this observation on?
7. How important do see the attributes (which are listed in 1 Tm 3:1-7 and Ti 1:6-9) to a man doing the job of an elder? Please explain your position.
8. Does the ability that an elder has to teach and preach have any bearing on how well the local congregation grows in its spiritual maturity? Has this had any affect upon the spiritual wellness of today's congregation?
9. Do the elders today receive the respect, love and affection that the elders in times past received? What do you base this observation on?
10. How much authority do you see the elders today possessing? What is this authority based upon?
11. When problems arise in your congregation who is called upon to address those problems? Why do you suppose that is?
12. When it comes to scriptural matters are the preachers or the elders the main source of information? Why do you see this as the case?

Interview Questions for Case Study
(Congregation with Elders)

1. How long has this congregation had elders?
2. How do you view the job of the elder, as shepherds or administrators?
3. Do you see a shortage of elders in the church today? What do you see as the cause of this shortage?
4. Is there a plan to replicate elders here? What is being done here to ensure that there is not a shortage of elders in the future?
5. How do you identify potential elders?
6. What is done to help those identified to mature spiritually for the job.
7. Have you seen a loss in eldership oversight today compared to the last century?
8. What has been lost in elderships today? What do you base this answer on?
9. To what extent do you see the need for communication with the congregation you serve?
10. What is the spiritual level of the congregation where you serve? Is it as strong as it was in the past? What is the basis for your answer here?
11. Do you see a place for men's business meetings? What is that place and how does it affect the eldership oversight.
12. Are steps being taken to edify the congregation here? What affects is this having on the congregation here?

Interview Questions for Case Study
(Congregation without Elders)

1. Has this congregation ever had elders?
2. How long has it been since there were elders?
3. What were the circumstances to the loss of the eldership oversight here?
4. Does this congregation desire to have elders? Why?
5. In your travels have you noticed a decline in eldership oversight? What do you base your answer on?
6. How do you view the work of an elder - as an administrator or a shepherd?
7. Is it scriptural for a congregation to not have elders? Please explain your answer.
8. Can a congregation be spiritually pleasing to God without elders?
9. Is there anything being done to build an eldership here?
10. What have elderships lost today in the ability to mentor the next generation of elders? What do you base this observation on?
11. How important are the attributes given by Paul in 1 Timothy 3, Titus 1, and 1 Peter 5:1-3 when it comes to the selection of men for the eldership?
12. What role does the minister have in the leadership of this congregation?
13. How is business conducted in this congregation?
    a. In matters of edification?
    b. In matters of evangelism?
    c. In matters of benevolence?
    d. In matters of administration?

Relational Skills Inventory

The following are some people skill-sets for leadership in general. Rate the level of each skill that you believe an elder should possess.

Skill	necessity	needed	not needed	neutral
1. Listening	_________	_________	_________	_________
2. Networking	_________	_________	_________	_________
3. Conflict Resolution	_________	_________	_________	_________
4. Decision Making	_________	_________	_________	_________
5. Risk Taking	_________	_________	_________	_________
6. Problem Solving	_________	_________	_________	_________
7. Confronting	_________	_________	_________	_________
8. Encouraging	_________	_________	_________	_________
9. Trust Building	_________	_________	_________	_________
10. Inspiring/Motivating	_________	_________	_________	_________
11. Team Building	_________	_________	_________	_________
12. Consensus Building	_________	_________	_________	_________
13. Recruiting	_________	_________	_________	_________
14. Hiring/Firing	_________	_________	_________	_________
15. Conducting Meeting	_________	_________	_________	_________
16. Rewarding	_________	_________	_________	_________

17. Questioning   _______   _______   _______   _______

18. Disagreeing   _______   _______   _______   _______

19. Confronting   _______   _______   _______   _______

20. Counseling   _______   _______   _______

21. Mentoring   _______   _______   _______   _______

22. Community Building _______   _______   _______   _______

23. Challenging   _______   _______   _______   _______

24. Trusting   _______   _______   _______   _______

25. Empowering   _______   _______   _______   _______

26. Evaluating   _______   _______   _______   _______

27. Managing   _______   _______   _______   _______

28. Leading   _______   _______   _______   _______

29. Delegating   _______   _______   _______   _______

30. Discipling   _______   _______   _______   _______

31. Evangelizing   _______   _______   _______   _______

32. Correcting   _______   _______   _______   _______

Appendix G:

Task Skills Inventory

The following are some task skill-sets for leadership in general. Rate the level of each skill that you believe an elder should possess.

Skill	**necessity**	**needed**	**not needed**	**neutral**
1. Preaching	_________	_________	_________	_________
2. Teaching	_________	_________	_________	_________
3. Researching	_________	_________	_________	_________
4. Communicating	_________	_________	_________	_________
5. Mission Development	_________	_________	_________	_________
6. Mission Casting	_________	_________	_________	_________
7. Vision Development	_________	_________	_________	_________
8. Vision Casting	_________	_________	_________	_________
9. Trust Building	_________	_________	_________	_________
10. Strategizing	_________	_________	_________	_________
11. Reflecting	_________	_________	_________	_________
12. Time Management	_________	_________	_________	_________
13. Use of Technology	_________	_________	_________	_________
14. Prioritizing	_________	_________	_________	_________
15. Writing	_________	_________	_________	_________
16. General Planning	_________	_________	_________	_________

17. Making Presentations   _________   _________   _________   _________

18. Praying   _________   _________   _________   _________

19. Budgeting   _________   _________   _________   _________

20. Counseling   _________   _________   _________   _________

21. Mentoring   _________   _________   _________   _________

Appendix H:

Record of Data Interviews

ID#: Identification number for each interview

PG: Permission granted for use of written comments –
    Y = yes, N = no

CP: Current Position within the church

SC: Size of congregation

ID#	DATE	STATE	PG	CP	SC
INT1	9/4/17	Texas	Y	Laity	60
INT2	9/4/17	Texas	Y	Laity	60
INT3	9/4/17	Oklahoma	Y	Minister/Laity	40
INT4	9/4/17	Texas	Y	Elder/Minister	750
INT5	9/5/17	Oklahoma	Y	Laity	100
INT6	9/5/17	Texas	Y	Laity	50
INT7	9/5/17	Texas	Y	Laity	750
INT8	9/5/17	Texas	Y	Laity	50
INT9	9/6/17	Oklahoma	Y	Minister	60
INT10	9/6/17	Oklahoma	Y	Minister	45
INT11		Texas	Y	Ex-Elder/Laity	40
INT12		Texas	Y	Ex-Elder's Wife/Laity	40
INT13	9/7/17	Oklahoma	Y	Laity	600
INT14	9/7/17	Oklahoma	Y	Laity	600
INT15	9/7/17	Oklahoma	Y	Elder	150
INT16	9/7/17	Oklahoma	Y	Elder's Wife/Laity	150
INT17	9/8/17	Texas	Y	Laity	75
INT18	9/24/17	Oklahoma	Y	Deacon	160

ID#	DATE	STATE	PG	CP	SC
INT19	9/24/17	Oklahoma	Y	Deacon's Wife/Laity	160
INT20	9/24/17	Oklahoma	Y	Laity	160
INT21	9/24/17	Oklahoma	Y	Minister	160
INT22	9/24/17	Oklahoma	Y	Laity	160
INT23	9/24/17	Oklahoma	Y	Laity	160
INT24	9/24/17	Oklahoma	Y	Laity	160
INT25	9/26/17	Oklahoma	Y	Laity	150
INT26	9/28/17	Oklahoma	Y	Laity	30
INT27	9/28/17	Oklahoma	Y	Minister	40
INT28	9/28/17	Oklahoma	Y	Minister	50
INT29	9/28/17	Oklahoma	Y	Minister	120

Church Leadership Interview Percentages

Question	Yes	Neutral	No
How do you view elders - as shepherds (S) or administrators (A)?	S 45%		A 55%
Is it important to have elders?	97%	3%	
Does your congregation have elders?	62%		38%
Is the church as spiritually strong today as it was in the past?	24%	3%	73%
Is there a desire to mentor the next generation of elders?	55%	7%	38%
Is it important to mentor the next generation of elders?	97%		3%
Is the elder's ability to teach and train today as strong as it was in the past?	31%	10%	59%
How important are the attributes of 1 Tim 3:1-9, Titus 1:6-9?	100%		
Does the elderships ability to teach and preach have an effect on the congregation's spiritual formation?	93%		7%

Question	Yes	Neutral	No
Are today's elders loved and respected as much as those in the past?	27%	21%	52%
What type of authority do elders have today? Yes = Only in matter of the church No = In matters of both the church and the personal lives of its members	31%	10%	59%
When problems arise in the church, who addresses those problems?	Elders 48%	Men 17%	Preacher 35%
When spiritual matters arise, who is the main source of information?	Elders 10%	Unsure 7%	Preacher 83%
How often do your elders meet? (all those who "knew" were elders, deacons, or preachers - even some elder's wives were incorrect)	Knew 37%		Unsure 63%

Church Leadership Survey & Interviews Observation

Survey Statements	Survey Answers	Interview Observations	Researcher Observations
The congregation I attend encourages daily, individual study of God's Word.	93% agreed, 7% disagreed	72% said the church is not as knowledgable today as in the past, 24% said it is, 3% were neutral	The laity today is not studying God's Word like it used to, therefore Biblical knowledge is declining
I believe a congregation with qualified men does not have to have an eldership to be pleasing to God.	10% agreed, 90% disagreed	97% of interviewees agreed that having elders is important, while 3% were neutral	Of the 9 *congregations* respresented in the study, 4 were without elders (and had been without for >10 years). 11 of the 29 *interviewees* were without elders
I believe Paul instructed all congregations to develop elders.	93% agreed, 7% disagreed	38% did not observe the mentoring or teaching of future elders, 55% said they saw the desire in their elders to mentor, while 7% were neutral	While 96% interviewed saw the need to mentor the next generation, only 2 of the 9 congregations represented had a program in place to train elders
I believe the eldership has Biblical authority to make decisions for the local congregation.	73% highly agreed, 27% agreed	59% believed the authority extends to the personal life of the laity, 31% said it only applies in matters of the congregation, 10% were neutral	31% took the position that elders should deal with problems of the congregation but not individuals' lives. The neutral 10% tended to feel the same way

Survey Statements	Survey Answers	Interview Observations	Researcher Observations
I believe elders today have as much Biblical knowledge as those of the 20th century.	50% agreed, 50% disagreed	59% did not think today's elders have the ability to teach and defend the Word of God as well as those in the past, 31% thought they have as much knowledge, 10% were neutral	93% saw the need for elders to be able to teach and defend the truth as a primary cause for the weakness of the church today, yet 82% said when spiritual questions arise they approach the preacher rather than the elders
Elders I know spend time teaching young men how to be good elders.	60% agreed, 40% disagreed	55% said they saw a desire in elders to mentor, 7% said they did not know if the elders desired to teach, while 38% said there is no desire	Only 2 congregations reported having any type of formal mentoring or teaching in place. It was also reported that interviewees thought some of the congregations (which were not represented) had programs such as Lads to Leaders.
Elders today are held up in high esteem.	80% agreed, 20% disagreed	The numbers changed in the interviews - 52% said elders are not respected like they were in the past, 28% said they are, and 20% were unsure	The interviewees offered an explanation: Nearly all stated that it depends on the attitude of the elder. If the elder is shepherding and viewed as a spiritual man, then he is respected. If he is acting as an administrator and not leading, then he receives little respect. That correlates to 52% of interviewees witnessing elders not fulfilling their Biblical roles.

Survey Statements	Survey Answers	Interview Observations	Researcher Observations
I believe elders today have the ability and desire to mentor the next generation of elders.	70% agreed, 30% disagreed	55% said that there is a desire and ability to mentor the next genera-tion, 38% said that there is no desire, and 7% were neutral	The majority of inter-viewees said mento-ring is being done by teaching classes and leading by example. Only 2 congregations represented had formal training or mentoring programs in place.
Men today have a desire to become elders.	37% agreed, 63% disagreed	During the case study interview with the elder-ship, it was noted that the hardest thing to find when looking for elders is men who desire the office. Those interviewed attributed this to what men see happening to the present elders and the abuse they take from congrega-tions	During the interview process, one of the main reasons for the lack of elders proved to be a lack of desire for the office. The case study of the congre-gation with elders revealed that the last time they selected men to serve, out of 600 members in the con-gregation only 2 were found who desired the office *and* had the Biblical attributes.
Elders today are known for leading a congregation in its spiritual growth.	60% agreed, 40% disagreed	Only 45% ob-served elders as being shepherds - feeding and lead-ing the flock. 55% saw elders acting as administrators	The failure to lead the congregation as shepherds is the root cause for many of today's failures in local congregations. When elderships act as administrators, the congregation usually has a disdain for the eldership and a lack of both spiritual and numerical growth is observed